ENCYCLOPAEDIA OF EMINENT THINKERS

VOLUME-XIII: M.A. JINNAH

Volumes by the same author

The Political Thought of ***Veer Savarkar***
The Political Thought of ***M.A. Jinnah***
The Political Thought of ***Mohammad Iqbal***
The Political Thought of ***K.B. Hedgewar***
The Political Thought of ***M.S. Golwalkar***
The Political Thought of ***Lokmanya Bal Gangadhar Tilak***
The Political Thought of ***Pandit Deendayal Upadhyaya***
The Political Thought of ***Gopal Krishna Gokhle***
The Political Thought of ***Maulana Abul Kalam Azad***
The Political Thought of ***Sir Syed Ahmed Khan***

About the Author

Dr. Jai Narain Sharma (*b.* 1951) is Professor and Chairman of the Department of Gandhian Studies, Panjab University, Chandigarh. He is also Hon. Director of Gandhi Bhawan; member of Board of Studies, Nagpur University, Nagpur and Mahatma Gandhi Kashi Vidyapith, Varanasi; member of Research Degree Committee of the Department of Political Science, H.P. University, Shimla: General Secretary of Indian Soviety of Gandhian Studies; and member on the Presidium of the Alliance for Sarvodaya. He regularly writes for leading newspapers, and has published more than hundred research papers in professional journals of repute. Dr. Sharma has many books to his credit including *"Gandhi's View of Political Power"*, *"Economics of Defence: A Study of SAARC Countries"*, *"Economic Thought of Mahatma Gandhi"*, *"Human Resource Management"*, *"Alternative Economics: Economics of Mahatma Gandhi and Globalisation"*, *"Power, Politics and Corruption: A Gandhian Solution"* and *"Research Methodology: The Discipline and its Dimensions.*

ENCYCLOPAEDIA OF EMINENT THINKERS

VOLUME THIRTEEN

POLITICAL THOUGHT OF M.A. JINNAH

Jai Narain Sharma
Professor & Chairman
Department of Gandhian Studies
Panjab University, Chandigarh

CONCEPT PUBLISHING COMPANY, NEW DELHI-110059

Cataloging in Publication Data—DK
Courtesy: D.K. Agencies (P) Ltd. <docinfo@dkagencies.com>

Encyclopaedia of eminent thinkers / K.S. Bharathi.
v. 11-15 ; cm. — (Gandhian studies and peace research series ; 11)
Vols. 11, 14-15 by Ashu Pasricha; v. 12-13 by Jai Narain Sharma.
Includes bibliographical references.
Includes indexes.
ISBN 13: 9788170226840 (set)
ISBN 10: 8170226848 (set)

1. Statesmen—India. 2. Political science—India. 3. India—Politics and government. I. Bharathi, K. S. (Kuduva Swamy), 1956- II. Pasricha, Ashu, 1967- III. Sharma, Jai Narain, 1951- IV. Series: Gandhian studies and peace research series ; 11.

DDC 954.035 22

ISBN -13: 978-81-7022-684-0 (Series)
ISBN -10: 81-7022-684-8 (Series)
ISBN -13: 978-81-8069-493-6 (Vol. XIII)
ISBN -10: 81-8069-493-3 (Vol. XIII)

First Published 2008

Published and Printed by
Ashok Kumar Mittal
Concept Publishing Company
A/15-16, Commercial Block, Mohan Garden
New Delhi-110059 (India)
Phones: 25351460, 25351794
Fax: 091-11-25357103
E-mail: publishing@conceptpub.com

DEDICATED
TO
THE SACRED MEMORY
OF
MY RESPECTED FATHER
LATE PANDIT SADHU RAM VAIKARNACHRIYA
(1913-2005)

PREFACE

Among the most difficult problems that scholars face arises, when knowledge of events following the period they are studying, leads to the unwarranted condemnation or adulation of historical figures. Some historical events are of such magnitude that their repercussions flow not only into the future but also back into the past: such repercussions affect study of the events themselves as well as the personalities involved. Indeed, it is at times difficult to divorce certain personalities from particular events when attempting to understand an earlier period. One instance of this phenomenon is the 1947 partition of the India and subsequent studies of Mohammad Ali Jinnah (1876-1948).

The events of 1947 were charged with emotions and remain so even now: families were uprooted and hundreds of thousands died as a virtual civil war raged along the proposed border regions. Muslim refugees poured into what was to become Pakistan while Hindus and Sikhs made the journey in the opposite direction. Indian politicians, who had fought for a united India, saw the sub-continent divided and conceded the existence of Pakistan, often only in the belief that the new state would not survive and would eventually crawl back into the Indian nation. For their part, the British, and particularly Mountbatten, desired a united India as Britain's lasting legacy to the sub-continent. By contrast, for Muslim politicians who had worked towards it, the creation of Pakistan was the achievement of an ideal, an independent Muslim state; to many, an 'Islamic' state. In the centre of this melee of emotion and conflict, stood Mohammad Ali Jinnah, the Quaid-e-Azam. This title was given to him by his arch rival Mahatma Gandhi seen by supporters and critics alike as the politician solely responsible for the creation of Pakistan, having virtually 'wrested' this new state from the British at the eleventh hour. Jinnah's role has made him the recipient of substantial criticism from some scholars, as well as adulation from others. The emotion surrounding him has been further fanned by continuing poor relations between the two independent states. Some scholars have generally portrayed Jinnah as a vain and arrogant man whose main ambition was personal aggrandizement. They place him within the scheme of the Raj's divisive tactics towards Indian nationalist politics, suggesting he was a collaborator of the British. Recently decodified correspondance by the British government indicating a close link between Jinnah and Churchill further substantiates this line of thinking. This correspondance also reveals that the British-Muslim realtionship and their dependence upon each other was an old one.

By contrast, others examine the decision to invoke Pakistan as the political aim of most Muslims, and assess when that aim became an inevitability. They usually place Jinnah within mainstream Muslim politics to demonstrate his consistent concern with the rights of the Muslim community. To a large extent, these approaches reflect the political and intellectual climate of post Partition India and Pakistan. While writing this volume, I have tried to follow the dictum of the noted British editor C.P. Scott, who wrote: "Facts are sacred; comment is free." I have tried to put the facts as objectively as possible before the readers and have not made any comment or derived any conclusion. The readers are free to interpret the facts according to their own points and draw their own conclusions.

Personal acknowledgments are no easy matters where so many have been kind. My special thanks are due to Professor S.L. Malhotra, Professor R.N. Pal, Professor N. Radhakrishnan, Dr. K.S. Bharathi, Dr. R.P. Dwivedi, Dr. A.D. Mishra, Professor B.R. Duggal, Professor Raj Bir Singh Yadav, Professor M.L. Sharma, Dr. Meena Dutta, Dr. Ashu Pasricha and Dr. Rashmi Sharma. Beyond that I can make only an all embracing salute to the galaxy of the scholars whose works I have consulted.

I am also grateful to Shri Ashok Kumar Mittal, my publisher, for his consistent zeal in the publication of this volume.

Chandigarh **JAI NARAIN SHARMA**

CONTENTS

Encyclopaedia of Eminent Thinkers Series

Vol. I. The Political Thought of **Mahatma Gandhi**/ *K.S. Bharti*
Vol. II. The Political Thought of **Nehru**/ *K.S. Bharti*
Vol. III. The Political Thought of **Rabindra Nath Tagore**/ *K.S. Bharti*
Vol. IV. The Political Thought of **Radhakrishnan**/ *K.S. Bharti*
Vol. V. The Political Thought of **Vinoba**/ *K.S. Bharti*
Vol. VI. The Political Thought of **Aurobindo**/ *K.S. Bharti*
Vol. VII. The Political Thought of **Jayaprakash Narayan**/ *K.S. Bharti*
Vol. VIII. The Political Thought of **Vivekananda**/ *K.S. Bharti*
Vol. IX. The Political Thought of **Ambedkar**/ *K.S. Bharti*
Vol. X. The Political Thought of **M.N. Roy**/ *K.S. Bharti*
Vol. XI. The Political Thought of **Dadabhai Naoroji**/ *Ashu Pasricha*
Vol. XII. The Political Thought of **Veer Savarkar**/ *Jai Narain Sharma*
Vol. XIII. The Political Thought of **M.A. Jinnah**/ *Jai Narain Sharma*
Vol. XIV. The Political Thought of **Tej Bahadur Sapru**/ *Ashu Pasricha*
Vol. XV. The Political Thought of **C. Rajagopalachari**/ *Ashu Pasricha*
Vol. XVI. The Political Thought of **Subhas Chandra Bose**/ *Ashu Pasricha*
Vol. XVII. The Political Thought of **Mohammad Iqbal**/ *Jai Narain Sharma*
Vol. XVIII. The Political Thought of **K.B. Hedgewar**/ *Jai Narain Sharma*
Vol. XIX. The Political Thought of **Bhagat Singh**/ *Ashu Pasricha*
Vol. XX. The Political Thought of **M.S. Golwalkar**/ *Jai Narain Sharma*

1

LIFE AND ACTIVITIES

Jinnah was born on 25 December, 1876, in Karachi, as an underweight child. He was named Mohammad Ali Jinnahbhai. He was the eldest offspring of Jinnahbhai Poonja. The names of other children were: Rahmat Ali, Maryam, Ahmed Ali, Shireen, Fatima and Bundeh Ali.

A dispute on Jinnah's date of birth arose out of a variety of school admission records. When Mohammad Ali Jinnah was born, there was no system of maintaining such records in the Karachi Municipality. In the records of Sind Madrassabul Islam, Ḳarachi, his age was recorded as 14 years, without mentioning the date of birth. After a stay in Bombay, he returned to Karachi and got readmitted in the same madrassa with the following details[1]:

Name	:	Mohammad Ali Jinnahbhai
Native Place	:	Karachi
Date of Birth	:	20 October, 1875
Caste	:	Khoja

When Mohammad Ali Jinnah got admitted to the Christian Mission School as a Standard VI student, the school register showed his date of birth as 20 October, 1875. He himself signed the application form as 'Mohammad Ali Jinnahbhai'.

He sailed for London in January 1893, where he studied Law. In the register of the Council of Lincoln Inn his age was mentioned as 19 years, and the Council accepted Jinnah's petition to change his name from Mohammad Ali Jinnahbhai to Mohammad Ali Jinnah. All these contradictions prompted M.A. Harris to write an article

'Quaid-e-Azam's Birthday' which was published in the Civil and Military Gazette of 5 September, 1954, to prove that Jinnah was actually born on 20 October, 1875.[2]

Sarojini Naidu, who was very close to Jinnah, in her preface to *Mohammad Ali Jinnah: An Ambassador of Unity* mentioned that Jinnah was born on 25 December, 1875[3]. From 1939, the birthday of Jinnah on 25 December was celebrated as a public event. Weekly *Anjuman*, Delhi wrote a letter to Jinnah on 30th April, 1946, to which he confirmed that he was born on 25 December, 1875 in the early morning.[4]

In his early years, Mohammad Ali Jinnahbhai was not keen on studies. He was taught Gujarati at home by a private tutor. He, subsequently, joined the local madrassa, went to Bombay for studies where Poonjabhai's sister Manbhai was living. That did not last long. After Mohammad Ali's return to Karachi, he learnt horse riding as his father had many horses.

Ultimately, at the young age of fifteen, the General Manager of Graham Trading Co. offered to appoint Jinnah in their London office as an apprentice for three years. Before leaving for London, Jinnah got married to Emi Bai, a Khoja girl of Paneli. She was only 14 years old. Jinnah's marriage with Emi Bai was not a decision taken by him. The match was made by his parents. A big marriage party went from Karachi to Paneli village. The marriage procession was led by drumbeaters, women joining the procession, singing Gujarati wedding songs and sprinkling rice on the way, which was a typical local Gujarati Hindu tradition. Emi Bai stayed behind when Jinnah went to England. Jinnah's pet name at home was Mamad. It is claimed that Jinnah's mother Mithibai had seen a rupee coin size birth mark on Jinnah's right sole and she interpreted this as a sign of Jinnah's rise in his career. "My son is destined to be a Raja," said Mithibai. Jinnah's palm was read by an astrologer, who too predicted a great future awaited Jinnah.[5]

In London, Jinnah led an austere life, minimizing his personal expenditure, and never indulged in activities not in tune with the family tradition. He spurned the offer of a kiss from his landlady's daughter Miss Drake on Christmas. This unique character of Jinnah remained throughout. Soon, he decided to become a barrister. He joined Lincoln's Inn. His wife Emi Bai died when he was in London. Subsequently, he heard about his mother's death while giving birth to Bundeh Ali. This shock was unbearable to young Jinnah. While in London, he often used to visit the British Museum for studies and attended the House of Commons to hear the speeches of famous politicians like Gladstone, Lord Morley, Chamberlain, Balfour and many others. He imbibed their style of parliamentary debate, which proved useful in the future.[6]

Jinnah was an inspired man from the beginning. He genuinely believed that he would become great. He told his first cousin Fatima Ganji Valji, before leaving for England: "I will return a great man from England and not you and the family, but the whole country will be proud of me"[7]. His father's business was not his cup of tea. Although he went to England to learn business management and tricks of the trade, soon he was attracted to barrister's gown. His love for Law was really love at first sight.

In England, he read Shakespeare and almost decided to join a Shakespearian theatrical company. But his father did not like the idea. This brief honeymoon with theatre did have a lasting effect. Acting was a part of his legal advocacy, as also public life. Like every Gujarati he was softspoken with a low pitched voice. Though the stage lost a budding actor, but through his charismatic personality he got for the Muslims of the Indian sub-continent a home land of their own. In public performances he resorted to 'histrionic gestures' at variance with his usual manner of speech and all these he must have derived from his youthful enthusiasm for 'amateur activity'.[8]

In London, Jinnah attended his law classes regularly and in spare time visited the Library or the House of Commons to witness parliamentary proceedings. Ascetic and austere, he never visited "pulsating Piccadilly Circus nor loiter in the notorious bye lanes of Soho or spend time in pigeon populated Trafalgar Square". He joined Lincoln's Inn because there, on the main entrance, the name of Prophet Muhammad was included in the list of the great law givers of the world.[9]

Jinnah returned to India in 1896 and for three years he was a briefless lawyer. His break came when he joined as a temporary Presidency Magistrate. That built up his reputation as a person who could decide complicated cases in a simple manner. "He was a meticulous magistrate with special care for legal details". After he relinquished that position, he soon became a highly successful lawyer. Otherwise cool and stony, Jinnah had a sense of humour and some of the anecdotes are worth recapitulating.

On one occasion, Justice Martin requested Jinnah to speak louder. Jinnah replied: "I am a barrister, not an actor." The judge again interrupted Jinnah to raise his voice. Jinnah said: "If you will remove that pile of books in front of you, you might be able to hear what I have to say". Once Chief Justice Davis found the courtroom crowded. He wanted the doors to be closed. Jinnah retorted that the doors of justice should be kept open.[10]

Justice Davar obtained knighthood after convicting Lokmanya Tilak to six years rigorous imprisonment. Jinnah genuinely believed that he obtained that honour by doing what the government wanted and considered the sentence as savage.[11] He boycotted the dinner held in honour of Justice Davar.[12] He was genuinely a great admirer of Tilak for the cause of Indian nationalism. He was not bitten by the religious bug at that point of time in his life.

He received highest regards from contemporary legal luminaries. "If to achieve the maximum result with minimum effort is the hallmark of artistry, Mr. Jinnah is an artist in his craft. He likes to get down to the bare bones of a brief; stating the essentials of a case his manner is masterly. The court room acquires an atmosphere as he speaks, juniors crane their necks forward to follow every movement of the tall, well groomed figure, senior counsels listen closely, the judge is all attention."[13]

By temperament and inclination, Jinnah was devoted to law and constitution. His subsequent agitation for Pakistan was largely based on legal and constitutional exposition of the case. "He was cold and unemotional, and apart from law and politics, he had no other interest... He never read a serious book in all his life. His staple food was newspapers, briefs and law books."[14] He never cared to maintain even a diary.[15]

He was extravagant in western dress, kept an English chauffeur and English staff when he remained in London for a few years after his wife's death and practiced law. As a Gujarati, he loved his curry and rice. The only game he played was billiards. He earned enough in his legal career to lead an independent life.[16]

In 1939, he prepared and executed his will. Fatima Jinnah was the main beneficiary, and he provided enough for his daughter Dina, and did not forget the Aligarh Muslim University which helped to lay the foundation for Pakistan.[17]

As a lawyer, he was superb in his arguments and faced senior lawyers with courage and conviction. One case deserves a special mention. Mirza Mehr Ali, a police officer of J&K, was sentenced by a lower court for five years for marrying a widow before the lady had completed the period of iddat, i.e. the period of three years. Under Islamic law, such a marriage is not legal. Jinnah appeared before the court with papers and brief. He just accepted the date and time of marriage as proved by the prosecution. He sprang a surprise by arguing that under Muslim Law the Christian calendar had no relevance. Under the Muslim Lunar calendar the marriage had taken place after a few hours of the end of the iddat. The prosecution case was just demolished by one piece of argument.[18]

The Bhopal Waqf case is another example of Jinnah's clean conception of law. A *waqf* was created by Gen. Obaidullah Khan for award of scholarships. After his demise, the heirs of the deceased revoked the waqf. The heirs of Gen. Obaidullah engaged Sir Tej Bahadur Sapru. The state engaged Jinnah. Sir Tej Bahadur Sapru argued for three days quoting from law books and rulings. On the fourth day of hearing, Jinnah appeared with a thin file and an Urdu book. Jinnah stood up and said that the court had no jurisdiction to hear and decide the case. He presented the Urdu book to the hon'ble judge to peruse. An old law of Bhopal debarred the courts to adjudicate all matters involving a sum of Rs. one lakh and above. Such cases were to be decided by the ruler himself. This particular act was neither repeated, amended or deleted. Sir Tej Bahadur admitted his defeat.[19]

Throughout his life, Jinnah's probity was indeed high. He did not allow Muslim League contestants to buy off the opposition candidates. As a lawyer, his fee was Rs. 500 per hearing. In one litigation which Jinnah had accepted, a client had deposited Rs. 5000 in advance. After the third hearing, the case was decided in favour of the client. The client was happy and forgot about his lump sum deposit. Jinnah called him and refunded Rs. 3500 which was due to his client.[20]

After demonetization of thousand rupee currency notes a smuggler proposed to deposit a million rupees as contribution to Muslim League. Jinnah refused the 'silver bullets' and told the smuggler to declare his hoarded wealth and pay the taxes and said: "We don't want an anna out of your black money". As Governor-General, he refused salary beyond rupee one.

To him, law was the same for a common man and him as Governor-General. His car would stop if there were a red light signal. To Bhutto who became the prime minister much later in early seventies, traffic light were for ordinary people, not for him. When some colleagues and friends demanded that he change his security officer. Since he was a Parsi he refured to do so.

Jinnah did not change his controversial lifestyle to impress the masses. He ignored all streaks of fundamentalism, at least when it came to his lifestyle. When he went to Simla to meet the Viceroy, he was wearing a white sola hat, which he refused to remove when requested by his Muslim supporters. He said, "I am not a hypocrite."[21] He was smoking a cigarette when he came out of the Legislative Assembly in New Delhi during the holy month of Ramadan, a month of fasting for the Muslims. When reminded of this, he gave the same reply.

But for achievement of Pakistan, he did resort to hypocrisy by making contradictory utterances. His greatest act of dishonesty was towards the Indian Muslims who were asked to fend for themselves after the creation of Pakistan. He did not sell his 'Bombay house, but his sister Fatima got an evacuee property in exchange of that house in Karachi. He made different promises to different interest groups to keep the Muslims united. His greatest hypocrisy was to deny his Hindu past in public, though he privately admitted that his ancestors were Rajputs from Punjab.

Political Life of Jinnah

Jinnah was closely associated with Dadabhai Naoroji. He initially joined the Congress. Gopal Krishna Gokhle was a great admirer of Jinnah and called him "the best ambassador of Hindu-Muslim unity". Such were his credentials—secular, modern and forward looking. Jinnah was set to soon capture the centre stage of Indian politics. He had even opposed in the beginning, the separate electorate demand of the Muslim League.

Soon, Jinnah realized that his style of politics had no place in India's independence struggle. His political space was squeezed out by Gandhi-Nehru combine. Thus, he drifted dangerously towards Muslim League. No one in Congress or in the country tried to stop this drift because he was being considered a nuisance by them. Many historians may dispute this, but events and happenings of that period indicate such a possibility.

Soon, the Muslims found an answer to their search for a leader who would give shape to their hopes and aspirations. The search stopped with Jinnah. He was elected President of the Muslim League in 1920 and continued to be in that position till 1930. Only from 1930 to 1936 he was not the President of the Muslim League because of the death of his wife. Thus, it is clear that Muslim League and Jinnah were one and the same. The second line of the Muslim League leadership was too feeble to engage Jinnah and others in a democratic process of discussion and debate. This explains why the democratic leadership failed in Pakistan soon after the death of Liaquat Ali Khan and subsequent imposition of martial law.

Jinnah's personal life remained a secret in the sense that he never communicated much to others, nor did he write about his personal life, unlike other Indian leaders who were too keen to keep everything on record. Liaquat Ali Khan also did not write much, nor did Adudur Rab Nishter and others. All of them were very educated. Why did they behave like that? Was it because they did not want to expose their private life for public scrutiny. Or was it because their writings would have invited a backlash from clerics and fundamentalists whose only agenda was creation of a homeland exclusively for Muslims and their intolerance of other faiths?

Jinnah married Rattanbhai (Ruttie) Petit, a love match, but strangely no document has surfaced to show how love grew between the 42 year old Jinnah and teenaged Ruttie.

In 1919, after one year of marriage, Jinnah's daughter Dina was born. Her name was not Islamic in the sense that it was more Parsi than Muslim. Her childhood days were lonely, specially after death of her mother early in her life. Jinnah during this period was lost and lonely, and went to London to get over from family tragedy, although his relationship with his young wife was already estranged. Dina married Nevillee Wadia, a Parsi turned Christian in 1938, two years before adoption of the Muslim League resolution of 1940.

Politics of Jinnah: A Chronology

In the year 1906, Jinnah launched his political career by attending the Calcutta Congress session as Secretary to the Congress President Dadabhai Naoroji. From 1906 to 1920 he was a nationalist, called himself as Indian first and then a Muslim. He was the president of the Home Rule League, and made stirring speeches in Shantaram Chawl, Bombay, which was the venue of political meetings. From contributions made by rich and poor alike they (the people) had built a hall, which they named after him. Jinnah Hall exists as an evidence of Jinnah's nationalism and India's tolerance as, despite the fact that he later became the architect of partition, India did not change the name of the hall.[22] Chagla remained with the Muslim League as long as Jinnah remained a nationalist.

Jinnah changed his stance gradually, came to the conclusion that the Muslims deserved separate electorate with reservations of seats at all levels "as a matter of necessity to the Mohamedans".[23] This was the basic demand since 1906 when the Muslim League was created. Pakistani historians like Sharif-al-Mujahid have emphasized the point that "without separate electorate, there would have been no Pakistan. The Congress accepted the principle of separate electorate under the Lucknow Pact, but soon realized the mistake and subsequently campaigned against it. If ever there is again a demand for separate electorate with reservations for the Muslims of India, there would again be subsequent demand for another division of India. This is what history has proved by the nature of Pakistan movement. Says Chagla: "If the basis of elections had been joint electorates, there would never have been a demand for separation or partition.[24]

The separate electorate politics of the Muslim League did not provide a type of Muslim rule even in Muslim majority provinces as they were mostly ruled by secular Muslim prime ministers/chief ministers with the backing of Hindu members. Thus, a strange demand was made by Jinnah to accept the Muslim League as the sole representative of the Muslims. This strategy paid windfall profits to Muslim League by winning majority Muslim seats in North India in 1945-46 election. The Muslim League, however, failed to obtain majority seats in the four provinces of the proposed West Pakistan in 1945-46 election. To achieve dominance, the Muslim League decided to call for 'Direct Action' to be launched from 16 August, 1946.

On 5 August, 1929 Jinnah considered Hindu Muslim question as a national problem. Ten years later, on 5 August, 1939 in a public meeting in Bombay he said that western democracy was not "suited to genius of India". The rule of the majority was perceived as a rule of Hindus. In an article published in *Time and Tide*, London, Jinnah explained that western democratic system was not in the interest of the Muslims. While introducing the Pakistan Resolution a year later in 1940, he said that Hindus and Muslims could never be a common nationality. Again in 1941 on 23 March he said "social and cultural differences would not permit Hindus and Muslims to rule (India) jointly".

Jinnah called upon the Muslims to join Muslim National Guards in 1942 "to meet any emergency for the Muslim cause". This was a turning point for relentless aggressive posture of the Muslim League, a preparation of bloody confrontation with Hindus. The Muslim National Guards eventually gave scope to Muslim ex-servicemen and this organization was in the forefront of implementing the Direct Action Programme that led to great Calcutta killings of 10,000 innocent people. In a similar fashion, the service organizations were eventually divided on communal basis like All India Railway Muslim Employees Association.

Jinnah's determination for creation of Pakistan was reflected in various speeches he made after adoption of the 1940 Resolution. Addressing the students of the Islamia College, Peshawar, in November 1945, he said: "We want to get rid of the British but we do not want the change of masters. Let three-fourths of India belong to Hindus where they can rule as they wish and let Muslims have one-fourth of India where they are in majority. Let us both be free. What is terrible about it."

Communal riots took place in Punjab, Bengal and Bihar in 1946. Jinnah was aware of the implications of the demand for Pakistan. In November 1946, in a press conference he bluntly proposed "exchange of population" to save minorities from communal atrocities. He thus jeopardized the lives of Muslims in India by offering them to migrate to Pakistan. In Pakistan, as M.C. Chagla said before the UN General Assembly, the minority problem was solved by ethnic cleansing.[25] There is hardly any Hindu minority population in West Pakistan.

On 3 June, 1947, the partition plan was accepted by Nehru, Baldev Singh and Jinnah. Jinnah's dream was fulfilled on 14 August, 1947 by creation of a separate Muslim state of Pakistan. He gave an unexpected secular speech on 11 August, 1947 wherein he said that in Pakistan "Hindus would cease to be Hindus, Muslims cease to be Muslims in political sense". It was too late to alter the communal situation. This part of the speech had been 'excised' from the official documents of Pakistan. Jinnah felt guilty for the Muslims left in India. He further created a problem for Muslims in India by assuring them to depend on Pakistan for their well-being and protection (18 August, 1947 Id message). In Id message he acknowledged that "it is the Muslim minority provinces in the sub-continent who were pioneers and carried the banner aloft for the achievement of our cherished goal of Pakistan"[26]. Ever since then, Pakistan never gave up the pan Islamic vision of India. Since 1947, the hate India campaign remained the official policy of the Pakistan establishment. The ISI's destabilization programme for India is linked to Jinnah's greater Pakistan vision which was nurtured by Ameer Ali and Chaudhari Rehmat Ali. When Gandhi was assassinated, Jinnah's message of condolence was that Gandhi was one of the greatest 'Hindu leaders' of the modern times.

While M.C. Chagla, much before partition, was told by Jinnah that after creation of Pakistan, Indian Muslims should fend for themselves, we have a different version from Aziz Beg who says that in the Council of the Muslim League meeting held in Karachi in December 1947 (after the creation of Pakistan) in which 300 members participated, 106 were from India. In the meeting Jinnah expressed his deep sympathy for the Muslims left in India and pledged to safeguard their interest. Jinnah said if the Council decided, he would return to India to lead the Indian Muslims, a hypocritical statement. He also said that there "must be a Muslim League in India". This was a case of doublespeak Jinnah.[27]

Jinnah was taken aback when Lord Mountbatten told him that in the event of partition as pleaded by Jinnah by a 'surgical operation', there would be a partition of Bengal and Punjab too. Jinnah was horrified and argued at length on the need to preserve the unity of the Punjab and Bengal. The same Jinnah at one time even floated the idea of exchange of population. This is another example of his doublespeak and lack of clarity on important issues.

The prime mover of the Pakistan movement did not spell out his political vision. He kept everyone guessing on the structural edifice of the proposed state of Pakistan. Before partition his efforts were to mobilize all sections of Muslims in India by avoiding specifics. Thus, he could draw in land owners, socialists, communists, businessmen, lawyers, Muslim intellectuals and the middle class. By his recourse to religion he could mobilize the Muslim religious leaders and the masses hypnotized by a dream of a pure land for the Muslims in the sub-continent. As rightly said by McGrath, "each League member was free to create his own image of what Pakistan would be".[28]

Jinnah became the founder Governor-General of Pakistan and did not allow Lord Mountbatten to become the common Governor-General of India and Pakistan. He did not provide in advance the framework of the type of democracy to be introduced in Pakistan. In 1947, while he was engaged in negotiations for dominion status, Jinnah noted on his pad: "Danger of parliamentary form of government (i) it has worked satisfactorily so far in England and nowhere else; (ii) Presidential form of government more suited to Pakistan".[29] As far as Jinnah's first poser is concerned, history has proved him wrong as India has successfully completed fifty-five years of democratic rule which includes more than half a century of parliamentary democracy. Without experimenting with parliamentary form of government with the prime minister as head of government, he started advocating a form of Presidential form of government. This he did in a speech in Baluchistan after the formation of Pakistan. Again he repeated the same before officers at Quetta Staff College and argued that in terms of Government of India Act, 1935, the executive authority flows from the Governor-General.

Jinnah not only gave his views on presidential system of government, but implemented it by crippling the powers of the prime minister. He told Lord Mountbatten that in Pakistan, "I will be the Governor-General, and the Prime Minister will do what I tell him".[30]

Not only this, Jinnah presided over cabinet meetings and the prime minister remained on the sideline. On 30 December, 1947 the docile cabinet passed a resolution that in the event of difference of opinion between the cabinet and the Governor-General, the views of the Governor-General would be final and binding. The cabinet appointments were made by him and not by the Prime Minister. On the same day the Cabinet resolved:

"That no question of policy or principle would be decided except at a cabinet meeting presided over by Quaid-e-Azam and in the event of any difference of opinion between him and the cabinet, the decision of the Quaid would be final and binding."[31]

On 11 August, 1947, the Constitution Assembly elected Jinnah as the President of the Assembly. Thus, the Governor-General also became the President of the Constituent Assembly, something unheard of in any democracy. What is more glaring was the fact that apart from being Governor-General, he also functioned as a cabinet minister by keeping some newly created ministries under his direct charge.

As Governor-General, Jinnah took public position on political issues. He was an absolute leader with absolute power. The Pakistan movement leaders did not object to this kind of arrangement, which went against the principle of democracy. As there was no opposition, there was no need for him to clarify his role.

The democratic experiment in Pakistan thus had a false start. This gave justification to Ghulam Mohammad, Iskander Mirza and

Ayub Khan to assert that the presidential system was more suited in an Islamic democracy. In a sense, Jinnah created a constitutional problem which has impacted on the future of Pakistan. Till today, Pakistan is yet to decide whether the country should have presidential or parliamentary system of government. Barring Nazimuddin and Fazle Elahi, all past presidents were drawn from the bureaucracy and the army temperamentally was in favour of a strong president with powers of dismissal of elected prime ministers. Jinnah failed to provide a clear constitutional solution to this problem. He, in fact, empowered himself with all the powers of the Governor-General, the Prime Minister, the President of the Constitution Assembly, an arrangement which continued till his death.

Like Jinnah, his protégé, Liaquat Ali Khan, did not appreciate the essence of democracy. In 1948, he got the Act of 1935 amended by incorporating Section 92A by virtue of which a provincial government could be dismissed. In 1949, he dismissed the Mamdot ministry in Punjab and did not hold elections for years. When a Muslim League candidate was defeated at Tangail in Mymensingh district in May 1949, he set aside the results. He firmly believed that opposition had no role in Pakistan. He said: "I have considered myself as Prime Minister of the League. I have never regarded myself as Prime Minister chosen by the members of the Constituent Assembly".[32] He held the view that "the formation of new political parties in opposition of the Muslim League is against the interest of Pakistan".[33]

That Jinnah, who is often described as the Salahuddin of the sub-continent, had expensive habits like owning a fleet of cars, staying in good and posh hotels, being well dressed in western attire, smoking expensive cigarettes, drinking costly whisky and eating good foods, did not produce a negative image in Muslim society. Akbar S. Ahmad explains that in the Muslim society "there is no tradition of a half clad *fakir* leading them to a great victory". Muslims look to a person of substance, a leader whose dress and deportment proclaim his or her '*shaan*' or glory. Muslims want their commanders and leaders to look like commanders and leaders—proud, dignified, with head held high. It is claimed that this high aristocratic style of Jinnah was a plus point in building his image in the minds of the Muslims. But was it really so? Even Fatima Jinnah had to discard her *sari* and appear in *salwar kameez* with *dupatta* all in the name of Islamic identity. In the contemporary age, Osama bin Laden does not lead a flashy life. He has emerged as a pivotal pan Islamic figure not only because of his acts but also because of his spartan lifestyle.

Being a Salahuddin for the Muslims, Jinnah remained throughout the supreme leader, not to be questioned or challenged. Thus, the Pakistan movement did not produce leaders that were needed to sustain democracy. The most that could be achieved in the Pakistan movement was to produce only provincial leaders while the Indian National Congress produced a host of national leaders.

Assessment of Jinnah

A study of Jinnah is a study of phenomenal growth of communal politics in the Indian sub-continent. His gradual shift to aggressive Muslim identification as a cornerstone of his ultimate call for creation of a Muslim homeland introduced a lethal poison in the Indian politics. Iqbal and Jinnah made it clear that the British India had two components 'Muslim India' and 'Hindu India'. This division was termed as being international in the Lahore session of the Muslim League and not inter-communal. Jinnah's speech on the occasion was clear on the subject. Says Rafiq Zakaria:

'The harm that Jinnah did is incalculable.... Even the worst Muslim ruler in the middle ages did not alienate the Hindus from the Muslims so badly as the so called Quaid-e-Azam had done.'[34]

He never revealed his true identity. Zulfikar Ali Bhutto was frank enough to admit that his forefathers had embraced Islam and they originally hailed from Rajasthan Rajput dynasty called Bhatis. Pakistani historians projected Jinnah as a Punjabi from Sahiwal district. He was a Shia, but posed as a Sunni for political reasons. For Pakistanis, he was a Salahuddin and a second Aurangzeb. For vast majority of Indians, he was the man who broke India into two. His present status has been vastly dented by the creation of Bangladesh. The Mohajirs now have rejected his two nation theory on the basis of their bitter experience of the reality of Pakistan.

There is no more cry for 'Jinnahpur' as their proposed land in Pakistan.

Jinnah is an example of how a non-practising Muslim, eating ham and drinking whisky, could emerge as Quaid-e-Azam, the supreme leader. Jinnah is the greatest contradiction of history. He put the Pakistani part of sub-continent behind by a century. The right parties in Pakistan are not enamoured of Jinnah and his legacy. Fazlur Rehman of the Jamaat once said, if Jinnah had a vision of secular Pakistan, why then did he divide India into two[35]. Such a controversy is now emerging in Pakistan as Jinnah had delivered in his 11 August, 1947 speech containing his vision of a secular Pakistan. Jinnah had told Reuter's correspondent in 1946 that the new state would be modern democratic state with sovereignty resting in the people and the members of the new nation having equal rights of citizenship regardless of their religion, caste or creed.[36]

In December 1946 Indian leaders were invited to London by the British government for discussion. At one such meeting Jinnah took aside Sardar Baldev Singh, and said:

'Baldev Singh, you see this match box. Even if Pakistan of this size is offered to me I will gladly accept it, but it is here that I need your collaboration. If you persuade Sikhs to join hands with the Muslim League, we will have a glorious Pakistan, the gates of which will be near about Delhi, if not Delhi itself.'[37]

Mountbatten concluded that Jinnah was a psychopathic case; "in fact, until I had met him I would not have thought it possible that a person with such a complete lack of administrative knowledge or sense of responsibility could achieve or hold ... so powerful a position."[38]

Pakistan was created out of bitterness and hatred and that continues even after decades of its creation.

Jinnah's concern for Muslims in India after partition was totally callous. He did promise protection even after partition, which was an absurd promise. Before partition M.C. Chagla raised this question before Jinnah. "You (Jinnah) are fighting for Pakistan mainly in the interest of the Muslim majority states. But what happens to the Muslims in the states particularly like Uttar Pradesh where they are in a small minority". Chagla said he would never forget the answer he gave. He looked at Chagla for a while and said: "They will look after themselves. I am not interested in their fate".[39]

Admittedly, Jinnah had certain qualities of heart and soul. He remained a faithful husband. After Ruttie's death, he never married again nor did he indugle in romance with any woman. He did not object his daughter being named Dina, a Parsi name. He, after initial objection, allowed Dina to marry a Bombay based Parsi. Jinnah was honest to the core, never drew salary as Governor-General of Pakistan. He was not emotional. He was a stickler for rules. He refused to meet one of his brothers just because he wrote in his visiting card that he was a brother of Jinnah. He was very particular about his dress. He rarely smiled, and maintained a stern exterior. He was a brilliant lawyer who could argue his case forcefully. He was a Muslim with no sectarian classification. He knew sectarian polarization would bring disaster, as it is happening now. Ahmed Ali Jinnah, brother of Jinnah living in Bombay, had told his Hindu friend in 1946 at the time of great Calcutta killings that his brother Quaid was not interested either in Islam or in Pakistan. His obsession was to become a badshah.[40]

Nehru, in his autobiography, said: "Temperamentally, he (Jinnah) did not fit in at all with the new Congress. He felt completely out of his elements in the khadi clad crowd demanding speeches in Hindustani."[41]

Often, it is asked what deep seated compulsion caused Hindus and Muslims to split the sub-continent which geography had formed into one unit? Jinnah believed and said that Pakistan "started the moment the first non-Muslim was converted to Islam" as his conversion to Islam made him a different entity in the society leading to a state of separateness as "Hindus and Muslims did not inter dine or inter marry". This was rather a simplistic explanation of a complex situation of Indian nationhood. He reverted back to composite Indian nationhood in his 11 August, 1947 speech after his election as President of the Pakistan Constituent Assembly. He said:

"You are free, you are free to go to your temples, you are free to go to your mosques or to any other place of worship in this state of Pakistan. You may belong to any religion or caste or creed that has nothing to do with fundamental principle that we are all citizens and equal citizens of one state. Now, I think we should keep in mind that in course of time Hindus would cease to be Hindus and Muslims cease to be Muslims, not in the religious sense, because that is the personal faith of each individual, but in the political sense as citizen of the state."[42]

Lord Mountbatten cited the example of Akbar as a model of tolerant ruler. Jinnah equated Akbar's tolerance to the Prophet who treated Jews and Christians equally after conquering them.

Jinnah remained an enigma. He did not speak in one language. He spoke different languages on different occasions to keep his divergent flocks together. In 1945 he told the correspondent of the Associated Press that "politically Pakistan would be a democracy". A few days later he told a religious leader that in the proposed state of Pakistan the laws will be consistent with the Shariat. Iskander Mirza, curious about Jinnah's ideas on the type of government he had in mind for the new country asked: "Sir, we are all agreed to go to Pakistan. But what type of government are you going to have? Are you going to have a government with the accent on Islam?" Said Jinnah: "No, nonsense, I am going to have a modern government".[43] On 11 August, 1947 he spoke, like Nehru did for India on the vision of a secular Pakistan. It was his political compulsion not to promote one consistent vision of the state of Pakistan. He got away with a variety of contradictory utterances on vital issues of the state. His early death saved him from further historical scrutiny. Having created Pakistan, he completed his personal mission of achievement. He wanted to prove equal to Gandhi and Nehru. Jinnah used the Muslim card for his political elevation. The Muslim rituals like praying five times a day were beyond his comprehension. It is a great mystery that such a person, deeply secular, caught the imagination of Indian Muslims as their Salahudin and Aurangzeb.

In the peak of time, Jinnah became Quaid-e-Azam, a title bestowed by Gandhi. Subsequently he became a modern Moses and, lastly, a Waliullah in the garb of a *jehadi* while championing the two nation theory. He was put on a pedestal as a diehard Islamist which he was not. Jinnah to *jehad* was the most logical culmination of his two nation theory, notwithstanding his secular views expressed on 11 August, 1947.

Last Days of Jinnah

Jinnah could not rule long after the creation of Pakistan. Dr. J.A.L. Patel, a Mumbai physician, was privy to Jinnah's terminal disease of tuberculosis and it remained a closely guarded secret. Had this been known to the British authorities or to Indian politicians, the course of history would have been different. His failing health was observed from 14 July, 1948. He was moved to Ziarat, Baluchistan. On 13 August, 1948 he was moved to Quetta on the advice of his doctor. From 5 September swelling developed on his feet with reddish spots on his frail body. On 9 September his condition further deteriorated. Finally, on 11 September he was moved to Karachi, reaching his residence at 6.40 p.m. He breathed his last at 10.25 p.m.[44] He was so dress conscious that during transit from place to place in ailing condition he insisted on wearing his western dress instead of the comfortable *pajama*. This version is disputed by Sri Prakash, the then Indian High Commissioner in Pakistan. According to him:

All the facts are not known and will never be known... It is quite clear that Mr. Jinnah did actually arrive in the Governor-General's special plane from Quetta to Mauripur, the military airport at Karachi ... nobody was even informed of his arrival. At Mauripur he appears to have been put in some sort of an ambulance van, which was in far from good condition. This broke down on the way as it proceeded to the Government House.... Many people thought he had actually died at Quetta. Anyway, it is clear that the Prime Minister and others were not told of his death till about midnight.[45]

Fatima Jinnah's version and versions of others need recapitulation. Fatima was nearest to Jinnah for more than two decades. Jinnah had problem of lung infection and cough from 1941. He used to smoke heavily. His favourite brand was Craven A, smoking 50 cigarettes a day, which he could not give up. He regularly used Waterbury's compound. The mass slaughter during partition did produce a guilt complex. He said on 30 October, 1947 in Lahore:

"Some people might think that the acceptance of the June 3 plan was a mistake on the part of the Muslim League" and blamed forces of disorder and disruption in the sub-continent causing the death of lakhs and enormous destruction of property. At the end in justification of deaths he said: "Our religion teaches us to be always prepared for death... There is no better salvation for a Muslim than the death of a martyr for a religious cause."[46]

It would appear that, apart from his ailment, the turmoil of partition did affect him emotionally. On 24 July, 1948 Dr. Col. Illahi Bux confirmed that Jinnah was suffering from tuberculosis, which fact was not made known to Liaquat Ali Khan when he came to Ziarat to enquire about Jinnah's health as that would be divulging a well guarded secret without the patient's permission.

On doctor's advice, he was brought to Quetta on 13 August, 1948. By the end of August Jinnah told Fatima that he had no interest to live. "The sooner I go the better!" This is corroborated by doctor Illahi Bux's version. Jinnah told him: "When you first came to Ziarat, I wanted to live. Now, however, it does not matter whether I live or die!" The doctor noticed tears in Jinnah's eyes. He had completely lost the will to live. The doctor gave enough indication that something had happened that "undermined his will to live!"[47]

In Quetta his health deteriorated steadily. His condition became serious. Again on doctor's advice, on 11 September he was flown to Karachi's Mauripur Airport at 4.15 p.m. He was kept on oxygen during the flight. There was no one at the airport to receive Jinnah, barring his military secretary, Col. Knowler. He was under instruction only to bring an ambulance along with a car. He was also instructed to keep everything secret. Jinnah was carried on a stretcher to the ambulance. The distance between the airport and the Governor-General's residence was 10 miles. The ambulance was made to travel at the speed of 5 miles an hour to prevent jolting the patient. One version was that the ambulance coughed up after travelling some distance. Col. Knowler reported that the engine of the ambulance got heated up due to slow speed. There was no spare ambulance as a standby. Col. Knowler had to personally go and fetch another ambulance.[48] "It is sadly strange that it did not occur to anybody that the Governor-General's car could tow the light weight ambulance". At about 8 p.m. the new ambulance arrived. Till then Jinnah remained in the ambulance, sweating and perspiring. The heat of Karachi was unbearable. Scores of flies were buzzing around his face. Jinnah's life was "ebbing away, drop by drop, breath by breath".[49]

At the Governor-General's residence there was no arrangement for a nurse, no local doctor or a patient's bed. It is unthinkable that the Head of the State remained without adequate medical assistance. Dr. Bux ordered a circulatory stimulant to be administered by mouth, but the patient could not swallow the medicine. Doctor Bux wanted to raise the foot of the bed and called for bandages for his legs to increase the flow of blood to vital centres. No one was available even to lift the foot of the bed and the doctor had to do it himself. The bed was extremely heavy and he succeeded to lift it by six inches but could not maintain it for long. He asked Fatima Jinnah to get some books to be used in place of bricks.[50]

By 9 p.m. Jinnah's pulse was failing. Dr. Bux administered an injection to revive his heart. Intravenous injection could not be given as his veins had collapsed. Jinnah was conscious. When doctor told him: "Sir, God willing, you are going to live!" Jinnah gave a startling reply: "No, I am not." After this he fell unconscious and his pulse stopped beating at 10.25 p.m. At the time of death only three doctors, a nurse and Fatima were there. When finally told of Jinnah's death, Fatima cried and collapsed.

Fatima Jinnah gave a different version at the time of death of Jinnah. After two hours of sleep, Jinnah opened his eyes, called Fatima and whispered, "Fati khuda hafiz" and uttered a *kalima*. His head dropped on the right side and eyes closed.[51]

On 12 September, 1948 the funeral procession started at 3.00 p.m. It was a state funeral under the command and control of the defence services. People in lakhs thronged the roadside and the burial ground. Everyone recited kalima. At 6.15 p.m. the funeral procession reached the final destination. The *namaz-e-janaza*, as per Sunni rites, was led by Maulana Shabit Ahmed Usmani. Some evidence has now surfaced that Shia rites were performed privately at the Governor-General's residence. Maulana Usmani did not forget to remind the people in his funeral oration that Jinnah "was the greatest Muslim after Aurangzeb".[52]

During his lifetime Jinnah was considered a *kafir* by the fundamentalists. After creation of Pakistan he remained an icon. The fundamentalists often blame him for the secular speech delivered on 11 August, 1947 in the Constituent Assembly. His two-nation theory was dead after 1971 when Bangladesh emerged as an independent country. He created a class of mohajirs in Pakistan. The mohajirs are the most oppressed class, compared to Punjabis who are more than fifty per cent in terms of population. The Punjabi domination of Pakistan has virtually liquidated the concept of one nation of Islam. Altaf Hussain, the most prominent mohajir leader declared in September 2000 in London that "partition of the sub-continent was a grave mistake".

History is cruel to facts. Jinnah's personal ambition took precedence over the political and geographical realities of the sub-continent.

REFERENCES

1. S.K. Data and Rajiv Sharma, *Pakistan from Jinnah to Jehad* (New Delhi: UBSPD), 2002, p. 35.
2. *Civil and Military Gazette*, 05-09-1954.
3. Sarojini Naidu (ed.), *Mohammad Ali Jinnah, An Ambassador of Unity*; His Speeches and Writings (Madras: Ganesh), 1918, Preface.
4. Syed Sharifuddin Pirzada, *Some Aspects of Quaid-e-Azam's Life*, Islamabad, National Commission on Historical and Cultural Research, 1978.
5. Aziz Beg, *Jinnah and His Time*, Islamabad, Babur and Amer Publications, 1986, pp. 101 103.
6. S.K. Data and Rajiv Sharma, *Pakistan from Jinnah to Jehad*, *op. cit.*, p. 36.
7. Shamim Ahmed, 'A Leaf from Quaid-e-Azam's *Life*', *Dawn*, 27 September, 1948.
8. Iqbal Singh, *Illustrated Weekly*, 12 October, 1952.
9. Aziz Beg, *Jinnah and His Time*, Islamabad, *op. cit.*, pp. 158 160.
10. Sharifuddin Pirzada, *Some Aspects of Quaid e-Azam's Life*, *op. cit.*, pp. 30, 31.
11. *Ibid.*, p. 32.
12. M.C. Chagla, *Roses in December: An Autobiography* (New Delhi: Bhartiya Vidya Bhawan), 1973, p. 14.
13. Frank Moraes, *Times of India*, 10 September, 1939.

14. M.C. Chagla, *Roses in December: An Autobiography, op. cit.*, p. 55.
15. Aziz Beg, *Jinnah and His Time*, Islamabad, *op. cit.*, p. 165.
16. Akbar S. Ahmed, *Jinnah, Pakistan and Islamic Identity* (Karachi: Oxford University Press), p. 9.
17. *Ibid.*
18. Aziz Beg, *Jinnah and His Time*, Islamabad, *op. cit.*, p. 196.
19. *Ibid.*, pp. 196-198.
20, *Ibid.*, pp. 34-35.
21. S.K. Data and Rajiv Sharma, *Pakistan from Jinnah to Jehad, op. cit.*, p. 42.
22. M.C. Chagla, *Roses in December: An Autobiography, op. cit.*, p. 78.
23. Al-Mujahid Sharif, *Quaide-e-Azam* (Delhi: Low Price Publications), 1993, p. 11.
24. M.C. Chagla, *Roses in December : An Autobiography, op. cit.*, p. 76.
25. *Ibid.*, p. 309.
26. Al-Mujahid Sharif, *Qaide-e-Azam, op. cit.*, p. 642.
27. *Ibid.*, p. 646.
28. Allen McGrath, *The Destruction of Democracy in Pakistan* (Karachi: Oxford University Press), 1972, p. 53.
29. *Ibid.*, p. 35.
30. Larry Collins and Dominique, *Freedom at Midnight* (New Delhi: Vikas Publications), 1973, p. 221.
31. Zaifullah Sayed and Samuel Baid, *Pakistan: An End Without a Beginning* (Delhi: Lancer International), p. 14.
32. *Dawn*, 9 October 1950.
33. Sulakshana Mohan, *Pakistan Under Musharraf* (New Delhi: Indian Publishers), 1999, p. 15.
34. Rafiq Zakaria, *The Man Who Divided India* (Mumbai: Popular Prakashan), 2002, Preface.
35. *The Friday Times*, Pakistan, 19 June 1999.
36. K.K. Bhardwaj, *Pakistan's March to Democracy and Liberalism* (New Delhi: Anmol Publications), 1996, Preface.
37. S. Gopal, *Selected Works of Jawaharlal Nehru*, Vol. I (New Delhi: Orient Longman), 1972, p. 338.
38. Rafiq Zakaria, *The Man Who Divided India, op. cit.*
39. M.C. Chagla, Roses in December: *An Autobiography, op. cit.*, p. 80.
40. *Pioneer*, 10 November, 2000.
41. Jawaharlal Nehru, *An Autobiography* (London: The Bodley Head), 1937, pp. 67-68.
42. V.P. Menon, *The Transfer of Power* (Delhi: Orient Longman), 1958, p. 40.
43. Humanyun Mirza, *From Plassey to Pakistan* (New York: University Press of America), 1999, p. 243.
44. Fatima Jinnah, *My Brother* (Karachi: Quaid-e-Azam Academy), 1987.
45. Sri Prakash, *Pakistan: Birth and Early Days* (New Delhi: Meenakshi Publications), 1956, p. 113.
46. Fatima Jinnah, *My Brother, op. cit.*, p. 14.

47. Aziz Beg, *Jinnah and His Time*, Islamabad, *op. cit.*, pp. 857-858.
48. *Ibid.*, p. 862.
49. Fatima Jinnah, *My Brother*, *op. cit.*, p. 37.
50. Aziz Beg, *Jinnah and His Time*, Islamabad, *op. cit.*, p. 865.
51. Fatima Jinnah, *My Brother*, *op. cit.*, p. 38.
52. Akbar S. Ahmed, *Jinnah, Pakistan and Islamic Identity op. cit.* p. 36.

2

HINDU-MUSLIM UNITY

Sarojini Naidu in her expressive language called M.A. Jinnah as "Hindu by race and Muslim by religion."[1] Larry Collins and Dominique Lappierre in their racy novel *Freedom at Midnight* wrote, "Indeed, had not Jinnah's grandfather for some obscure reason become a convert to Islam, the two political foes (Gandhi and Jinnah) would have born in the same caste."[2]

It is very significant to note that till his transformation, Jinnah never allowed religion to dominate his political outlook or activity. He hated casteism and also rituals in Hinduism. It would not be out of place to quote Aga Khan. Jinnah belonged to his sect. Aga Khan compared Jinnah with Mussolini and wrote, "Each of them between his youth and his prime, travelled from one pole of the political opinion to the other. Each had one guiding light, whatever the policy, whatever the political philosophy underlying it, it would be successful and it would be morally justified, so long as he was at the head of it and directing it. In the view of both Mussolini and Jinnah, opposition was not an opinion to be compromised or negotiated, it was challenge to be obliterated by their superior strength and sagacity.[3]

Evidently, Mohammad Ali Jinnah was neither a moralist nor a religious leader. He began his political career as an ardent nationalist with a deep and sincere commitment to secular democracy. He abhorred religious obscurantism and sectarian politics, until he discovered a new destiny for himself in the evening of his life. It is stunning because he was a man who dedicated his youth for some definite ideals and revolted diametrically opposed in the evening of his life. Jinnah disliked mullahs so much so that he appointed a

Hindu, Jogindarnath Mandal as the first Kazi of sovereign republic of Pakistan. Most of Jinnah's intimate friends were Hindus and Parsis. Gokhale was his political guide, friend and philosopher. His ambition was to become a "Muslim Gokhale"[4]. He was destined to come into conflict with another celebrated disciple of Gokhale named Mohandas Karamchand Gandhi and this conflict was to decide the fate of Gokhale's country in such a way that Gokhale, though their Guru, could never ever have imagined this in his wildest dreams.

Congress was the best organised political party at that time and no wonder young M.A. Jinnah was attracted towards it. By then, Congress was visibly divided into the Moderate Congress and the Extremist Congress. But one thing was clear that no one could dominate public mind standing outside the Congress party. Jinnah's political career, its beginning and the way it ended, offers a very interesting and stunning case in history. He had been active in various other forums like Bombay's Anjuman-i-Islam since 1897. His formal public political career began with his election to the Bombay Corporation. He became active in the Bombay Presidency Association (BPA). He was destined to get involved in the Bombay branch of the Indian National Congress.

It was natural that Jinnah joined the Indian National Congress (INC) that had pledged to make India self-governing and the method was constitutional reforms. He attended the 28th annual session of Congress at Bombay's Oval Maidan in 1904. Sir Henry Cotton presided over this session, the then fiery imperialist Viceroy Lord Curzon who was the inspiration for another disastrous imperialist Churchill, had given a patronising advice that the salvation of India was not to be sought in the field of politics. Jinnah heard his role model Phirozshah roar, "How can these aspirations and desires be even gradually achieved unless we are allowed to play at all times a modest and temperate part on the field of politics?"[5] Surely, Jinnah in his heart knew that his attending of this session meant his joining the Congress. The political climate in England was favouring the Liberals and it had raised Jinnah's spirits. He expected concrete constitutional reforms for India.

But Jinnah had no liking for making the Congress a mass based party and failed to appreciate extremist thinking sparked off by

Hume and Hyndman. Jinnah's allegiance to the then creed, policy and programme of the Congress, is well recorded. Jinnah was destined to contribute a lot to the Indian National Congress before seeking its very destruction.

In March 1906, in search of his new destiny, he resigned from the Bombay Corporation and went ahead to Calcutta Congress of 1906 as a delegate. Jinnah's all India political career began as a Congressman. He became the private secretary to Dadabhai Naoroji, then the President of Congress. Most significantly, while Jinnah was rising high in the Congress echelons, the same year of 1906 saw the birth of All India Muslim League in Dacca (Dhaka). This was a party founded with profound blessing of the British by the top castes and classes like the landlords and aristocrats for their narrow selfish ends. The major purpose was to stop young Muslims from joining the Congress which was rapidly spreading, causing definite worry to the Government. The British policy makers were in search of a force that would contain the growing influence of the Indian National Congress wherein the extremist thinking was gaining ground.

It is very important to note that Jinnah did not join the Muslim League which he could have very easily done. The future Quaid-e-Azam would take seven years to formally join the League. There were definite convictions which held young Jinnah in the Congress party. Significantly, at that time the INC was not a political party as such but was more of a national expression of the people of India. It was a definite expression of the awakening nation. That is why there were no distinctive features and all people considered it natural to join the Congress. As even extremists could be accommodated within the Congress; the need for a separate party organisation was not felt.

The first phase of Jinnah's political career was essentially a Congress dominated period from 1906 to 1920. His socialisation held him close to the Congress. Top leaders like Naoroji had influenced him deeply in his formative period. Besides, in Bombay Presidency Association there were many Congress stalwarts such as Badruddin Tyabji, Gopal Krishna Gokhale, Sir Phirojshah Mehta, Sir Dinshaw Wacha among others with whom Jinnah was professionally and personally associated. His mercantile Khoja community was naturally closer to the Parsis who held eminent share in the commercial world of Bombay. This must have brought him closer to the Congress. He had handled many mercantile cases belonging to the Parsis. Jinnah had so deeply got involved in the affairs of BPA that in early 1905 he was sent along with Gokhale on a Congress deputation to England to plead for self-government for India during the impending British elections. Significantly, this must have been a deeply influencing event as Jinnah had personally seen Dadabhai's elections to the British Parliament and must have felt confident to secure something concrete from the British in terms of initiating political reforms in India. He must have agreed with Hume's ultimate vision of full self rule for India on the lines of the dominion of Canada.

Jinnah had the natural spirit of competitiveness and he moved an amendment to A. Choudhari's resolution on competitive examinations and reforms in Calcutta Congress of 1906. Jinnah objected to the application of 'reservation' clause for the 'backwardly educated class' of Muslims and asked that the Mohammedan community be treated in the same way as the Hindu community.[6]

The Surat Congress of December 1907 saw the open conflict between the Moderates and the Extremist. One member of the Extremist threw his shoe at the Moderate leader Sir Phirozshah Mehta. This resulted in a split in the Congress. The Extremists were expelled from the Congress. Self-government within the empire was declared the goal of the Congress. Significantly, Jinnah was also present. In November 1909 came the Indian Councils Act which enlarged the Viceroy's executive council with the addition of 35 nominated members and 2 elected members. It now became the new Imperial Legislative Council. Its members as elected representatives of the people had the right to criticise, and promote the government of their country. This saw M.A. Jinnah's election to the Council as the choice of the Muslims from Bombay. With this began Jinnah's ascent to power at the age of thirty three.

Jinnah was of the convinced opinion that if various communities of India could demonstrate a united front to the administration in their political demands, he felt such demands could not be refused. The strength of the Government of India was a consequence of various divisions in Indian society and, regrettably, in the specific division between the Hindu and Muslim communities. To extract concessions, political India had to work to bring 'about immediate cooperation ... and ultimate unity of purpose ... which is the only key to the future regeneration of our motherland under the British Crown.'[7] To bring about this goal he attacked the root causes of communal conflict, working with students to break down the barriers of communal distrust by advocating the development of inter-communal friendships as a student's patriotic duty. In June 1913, he was a founding member of the London Indian Association; the primary aim of this organization was: 'To maintain and foster unity, and to strengthen and encourage friendship between the Indian students in the United Kingdom[8] . . .' Jinnah stressed that it was the students' 'first duty while they were in this country to meet and understand their own countrymen'.[9] Later he participated in a meeting of the Bombay Muslim Students' Union and advocated a similar approach appealing to them to understand the other religious communities in India. 'That would be the surest way of progress in the country.'[10] Indeed, he argued, 'unity was absolutely essential to progress'.[11]

At the national political level, Jinnah had already brought Congress and the Muslim League closer through the adoption of similar goals. He now aimed to bring the two organizations together in a formal pact by focusing the attention of political India on the question of unity. By the time of his return to India, however, the war had changed the situation and created new problems for Hindu Muslim unity. The declaration of war by the British had given rise to the sentiment that India's loyalty to the British crown at this time should not be compromised by political agitation, however constitutional a form that might take. Further, the declaration of war by Turkey on the side of Britain's enemies was testing the loyalty of Indian Muslims, and many older Muslim leaders were fearful of holding political meetings that might provide a forum for the expression of pan Islamic themes. As a result, the December 1914 meeting of the Muslim League had been abandoned.

The government was well aware of the difficulties caused by the war with Turkey. In the months before Turkey's declaration of war, Hardinge attempted to keep the strained relations between England and Turkey a careful secret from Indian Muslims and had urged the home government to allow Turkey to act first.[12] In fact the British were sufficiently concerned over the effects of their war with Turkey on the loyalty of Indian Muslims to seek assurances from their allies on the sanctity of Islam's holy cities. Soon after the Turkish declaration of war, the viceroy was able to reassure Indian Muslims that the holy places of Islam were to be unmolested.

"In view of the outbreak of the war between Britain and Turkey... the Viceroy is authorized to make the following public pronouncement in regard the Holy places of Arabia, including the holy shrines of Mesopotamia and the port of Jeddah, in order that there be no misunderstanding on the part of His Majesty's most loyal Muslim subjects in this war ... These holy places and Jeddah will be immune from attack or molestation by the British naval or military forces ... the Governments of France and Russia have given similar assurances."[13]

In the final analysis, British fears over the loyalty of India's Muslims during the war years proved largely groundless. Although an undercurrent of dissatisfaction among the Muslim community remained, protest against Britain's war with Turkey was restrained by the decision of the Afghan king, Habib Ullah, to remain neutral throughout the war. Well aware of the relevance to Indian Muslims of the Afghan king's decision, the British were careful to ensure his neutrality.[14]

To bring Congress and the League together, Jinnah had to refocus Muslim concerns on the internal political scene rather than the wider international issues that war had brought forth. He felt it necessary to demonstrate the unity of the Muslim community as a whole to both Hindus and the British. Without cohesion within the Muslim community, as well as unity with Hindus, his dream of a united front against the British was undermined. Similarly, he desired to work within the Congress to unify its diverse factions. He laboured particularly to bring about the return to the Congress fold of the extremists who had quit the Congress in 1907 under the leadership of Tilak. In the case of divisions within the Muslim community itself, Jinnah chose to gloss over any suggestions of factionalism. In 1913 he argued that: "among the Mahomedans there is no such thing as 'split' . . . I would make bold to say the Musalman community was never more united or at one on all the fundamental questions of policy and principle than it is today. Differences of details there are and will be as you find all over the world amongst the most highly organized nations ... [it would be] a very unique community indeed consisting of 70 millions of people if there were no such differences."[15]

In fact 'differences of details' can only be described as a mild and politic description of the factionalism which existed within the Muslim community.

The primary difference was between the so called 'Young party' and 'Old party'.[16] The latter group represented those more conservative Muslim followers of the late Sir Syed Ahmad Khan who were suspicious of too close a tie with Congress. It saw loyalty to the British as the best method for their advancement and included in its membership Viqarul Mulk and Syed Mahomed Ali. The young party's most prominent members included Jinnah himself, the Raja of Mahmudabad, Mahomed Ali and the League secretary, Wazir Hasan. These younger nationalists desired to unite the League with the Congress in the common goal of self-government for India. Jinnah and his allies were initially unsuccessful in their attempts to unite the Muslim community in the pursuit of one consistent policy. They were, however, able to gain control of the Muslim League and, consequently, the Muslim political arena at the national level throughout 1915 and 1916. The aims of the young party were assisted by British policies towards Turkey and by the revocation of the partition of Bengal in 1911. Critics of the eventual pact between Congress and the League characterized it as 'merely one of the symptoms of Muslim dissatisfaction and discontent dating from the 12th December 1911[17]. Notwithstanding these contributing factors, Jinnah and his colleagues found that although they could not deliver a Muslim community whose facade was devoid of cracks they could at least demonstrate to Congress that their own views were dominant.

Within the Congress, Jinnah worked to engineer the return of extremists to the fold, this task being made easier by the apparent change of heart on the part of Tilak, who now indicated his preparedness to work within the constraints of constitutional politics to achieve the goals of Indian nationalism. His extremist followers were also now referred to under the more acceptable title of 'Nationalists'.[18] Gokhale remained wary of the views of Tilak and his followers and thwarted Jinnah's aims by deferring consideration of their re-entry at the 1914 Madras Congress session. Gokhale told Tilak that given his 'views and intentions it was clearly best that . . . [he] should remain outside the Congress'.[19] Earlier, Gokhale warned Annie Besant of Tilak's strength, and that any struggle to 'Put him down' would not be 'an easy fight'[20]. Gokhale's death in February 1915 smoothed the way to re-entry of the extremists the following year. Jinnah cast his net wide in this period in his unrelenting search for support for unity between Hindus and Muslims. While presiding over a meeting of the Gurjar Sabha in January 1915 to welcome the return to India of Gandhi from South Africa, he impressed upon Gandhi the importance of such unity. The South African question, in which Gandhi had been so actively involved, was to Jinnah the first issue 'on which the two sister communities stood together in absolute union'.[21] And, it was that frame of mind, that state, that condition which they had to bring about between the two communities, when most of their problems.... would be easily solved. That ... was one problem of all the problems of India, namely how to bring about unanimity and cooperation between the two communities so that the demands of India may be made absolutely unanimously.'[22]

The groundwork for political agreement between Congress and the Muslim League had been laid by 1913 with the tacit acceptance of separate electorates by Congress and the enunciation of the goal of the self-government by the Muslim League. What remained was for this great promise to be brought to fruition. To do this, Jinnah aimed to bring Congress and the League together in one city for their 1915 annual sessions. Under the influence of the prominent political activist Annie Besant, Congress indicated early in the year that its annual would be held in Bombay. Jinnah was left with the task of convincing the League of the benefits of also convening its annual session in Bombay. At Jinnah's insistence, a letter inviting the All India Muslim League to Bombay was circulated among members of the Provincial League as well as to other prominent Bombay Muslims for signatures, and then forwarded to the League Secretary, Wazir Hasan[23]. The controversy which arose out of this action was indicative of the divided views within the Muslim community in Bombay. Fazulbhoy Currimbhoy, who had himself been a signatory to the letter of invitation, complained that Jinnah had not been entitled to send the letter without the unanimous support of all the Bombay Muslim League members. He argued that Jinnah had tricked the Bombay Muslim Leaguers into signing the letter by stating that it would not be sent unless it was signed by all members. Currimbhoy wrote to Wazir Hasan at the same time of the 'inadvisability of holding the next session in Bombay.[24] Jinnah himself was quite prepared to override any opposition from within Bombay and indicated clearly that the 'Council of the League has the full power to hold the session of the League anywhere they may think proper'.[25]

The split in the Bombay Muslim community and the Provincial Muslim League paralleled that in the all India organization between the older, more conservative Muslims and those who were younger and more nationalistic. The former group wished to avoid any action which might be seen as disloyal by the British while the latter saw no reason to refrain from pursuing political reforms during a time of war which they assumed would be to their advantage. However, the Bombay situation was exacerbated by the intra communal conflict which existed within the city's Muslim community. Bombay had been rocked by Sunni-Shia riots during 1910 and tensions remained high. Most of the opponents of the meeting were either Khojas or Sunnis, while its supporters were predominantly Shia. Jinnah himself was seen by many Khojas as a traitor, having been born a Khoja who converted to the Shia faith.

In the final analysis Jinnah's view that the League should convene in Bombay held sway. He convinced the Aga Khan of the appropriateness of the League and Congress meeting in the same city and the Aga Khan subsequently wrote to Currimbhoy expressing his support for Jinnah. The Aga Khan had long indicated his desire for a 'permanent political sympathy and a genuine working *entente cordiale* between the members of the two great sister communities'.[26] Like many Muslims, though, he doubted the wisdom of holding political meetings during the war years and it was only after persuasion from Jinnah and Wazir Hasan that he agreed that grounds existed for immediate negotiations with Congress. As head of the Khoja sect, the Aga Khan's support at this time was crucial to Jinnah's cause. However, debate over the prospective meeting remained constant, with a war of words between the two sides being carried on in the press almost up until the date of the meeting.[27]

Surprisingly, it was the Governor of Bombay, Lord Willingdon, who stepped in and organized a truce between the warring Bombay Muslims. Jinnah had already corresponded with Cassam Mitta in an attempt to reach a compromise which would allow the Bombay session to go ahead uninterrupted and had assured Mitta of the continued loyalty of the League to the government.[28] In early December, Willingdon presided over a meeting of the protagonists in an effort to reach agreement.[29] A compromise emerged which required the meeting to pass a motion of loyalty to the government and on that basis a truce was arranged.[30] This was much to the chagrin of other British officials, who were opposed to any potential agreement between Congress and the League and expressed doubts over Willingdon's actions. It soon became apparent that the agreement between the two groups was superficial, and controversy surrounded the opening sittings of the League meeting.

The second sitting was disrupted by a large group of dissidents. Although a signatory to the Willingdon agreement, Cassam Mitta led the protesters and argued that the agreement had been broken by Jinnah and his cohorts. During the proceedings the session president, Muzhurul Haque, was abused by the dissidents for his English dress and for conducting the proceedings in English and not Urdu. The sitting was eventually adjourned when it became apparent to Jinnah that little could be achieved in the prevailing atmosphere. The next sitting was held in the Taj Mahal Hotel with only League members and members of the press in attendance. A resolution was passed at this meeting forming a committee to formulate and frame a scheme of reforms with other political organizations.[31] The Congress session endorsed a similar resolution for a committee to 'confer with the committee that may be appointed by the All India Muslim League', to plan a joint scheme of reforms.[32] It was these committees that eventually negotiated the terms of the Lucknow Pact.

Apart from the political stature gained by uniting Muslim India behind the League, he also intended to negotiate a new pact between the League and Congress. While he had foregone direct involvement in Congress, he had not lost his dream of uniting the two parties on a constitutional platform. During his presidential address he argued the cause of unity.

"We must not forget that one essential requisite condition to achieve Swaraj is political unity between the Hindus and the Mohammedans; for advent of foreign rule, and its continuance in India, is primarily due the fact that the people of India, particularly the Hindus and Mohemmedans, are not united and do not sufficiently trust each other; domination of the bureaucracy will continue so long as the Hindus Mohammedans do not come to a settlement. I am almost inclined to say that India will get Dominion Responsible Government the day Hindus and Mohammedans are united. Swaraj is an almost inter-changeable term with Hindu Muslim unity."[33]

To achieve his goals, he aimed to re-establish the Muslim League as the primary representative of Muslim India and then to negotiate an agreement with Congress on an equal basis.

An opportunity for agreement came with the holding of an All-Parties Conference in Bombay during December 1924, and in Delhi during January 1925.[34] Jinnah, however, did not view the conference as a suitable vehicle for agreement. He was wary of becoming too heavily involved in a conference that he saw as the brainchild of Gandhi. To involve himself with the decisions of Congress through participation on the All-Parties Conference Committee would only undermine his negotiating position. He only took up a position on the committee with the proviso that issues would not be voted on and all decisions must be unanimous.[35] In the event, the Conference Committee was adjourned indefinitely at the January meeting in Delhi after an impasse was reached.[36] The dispute was primarily between Jinnah and the more nationalist Hindus, Lala Lajpat Rai and Chintamani. Jinnah's request for Muslim majorities in Bengal and the Punjab was followed immediately by a lengthy rebuttal by Lajpat Rai.[37] Soon after, Chintamani indicated that any decision of the conference would have to be approved by the Mahasabha. The general response to Jinnah's demands was unguarded hostility and Jayakar suggested to his increased demands for separate representation that 'It appeared that appetite had grown by what it had fed on.'[38] It is clear that the Mahasabha had no intention of making compromises with Muslim India and while it remained a small grouping, it was very vocal and its leaders were able to present their views strongly. Its opposition proved to be effective and, after the committee's adjournment, Jinnah ceased to take an interest in it, turning to more direct negotiations with the Congress.[39]

At the Lahore Muslim League session, Jinnah had proposed the formation of a committee to negotiate with the AICC for a common approach to the political problems of India. This joint committee was to draw up a new constitution as well as a practical programme for the organization of workers and peasants.[40] The work of this committee was disrupted however by the machinations of Mahomed Ali, who was attempting at this time to rejuvenate his flagging political career. He and his brother Shaukat Ali vehemently opposed the revival of the Muslim League under Jinnah and throughout 1924 Mahomed Ali and Jinnah carried out a heated exchange in the press. In trying to maintain the position of his now almost defunct Khilafat organization, Mahomed Ali attacked both the validity of the Muslim League and that of Jinnah personally.[41] Jinnah returned the criticism in kind and questioned the respectability of the Ali brothers. He spoke disparagingly of Shaukat, suggesting that 'this little Maulana for the last three years has been making an annual attempt to destroy the Muslim League.'[42]

Although Mahomed Ali failed in his attempts to destroy the Muslim League and prevent Jinnah's domination of that organization, he was able to sabotage Jinnah's attempts to negotiate with Congress. As Congress president, he was able to orchestrate the Congress response to Muslim League overtures and subsequently affect the possibility of joint 1924 sessions of the League and Congress. Congress elements that opposed an alliance with the Muslim League were only too willing to use Mahomed Ali as a scapegoat for the breakdown in relations between the two organizations. When the Muslim League officially approached Congress, League members were upset by the response they received: 'Some of the members of the Council were so ruffled by the contemptuous treatment with which the Secretary of the Congress treated the request of the Muslim League Constitution Committee that it rejected the suggestions of holding the session at the same place where the Congress Session is going to be held.'[43] The Congress secretary referred to in this correspondence was Jawaharlal, Gandhi's fervent supporter, who had his own plans for Congress and saw Congress as the leading party in Indian nationalist politics, which precluded equal partnership with the Muslim League.

When Motilal heard of the Muslim League decision to hold its session separately, he moved quickly in an attempt to save the situation. In a telegram to Jinnah he appealed to him to bring the Muslim League to Belgaum, suggesting that the Swaraj Party would warmly welcome all parties to the session.[44] Jinnah refused to alter the location of the Muslim League session but in deference to Motilal postponed the session so that delegates might attend both Congress and League sessions.[45] Significantly, Jinnah himself did not attend the Congress session. The work that was begun by Mahomed Ali was eventually completed by elements within Congress that opposed making the concessions necessary to the Muslim community, for the achieving of a Hindu-Muslim accord.[46] Although both Motilal and Gandhi were enthusiastic about an agreement between the League and the Congress, Jinnah's plan to create a new Lucknow Pact remained just a dream. From the beginning of 1925, the rift between the leadership of the two organizations widened and was reflected in the disintegration of the Nationalist Party in the assembly.

Jinnah's immediate reaction to the breakdown of talks between the League and Congress was an attempt to create a new party outside the assembly, of politicians who were committed to the use of constitutional methods to attain political advance for India. In May 1925 he wrote to Jayakar indicating the need for a new organization, at least in Bombay. He argued that 'national interest demands the enunciation of a common policy which will offer a basis for the cooperation of all nationalists, irrespective of their party lable'.[47] Essentially, he was attempting to attract Indian politicians from both the Swarajist and Liberal parties, as well as the Muslim League, who continued to advocate a policy of 'honourable co-operation.'[48] In doing so, he hoped to strengthen his own position in Indian nationalist politics and undermine the position of Gandhi and the advocates of non-cooperation.

The programme of this new organization was clearly laid out.

1. A vigorous prosecution of a broad-based constructive programme through legislative and independent efforts.
2. The co-ordination of activities within the legislatures and public bodies and in the country.
3. The pursuit of a policy of opposition or support of measures as national interests demand a consideration of their intrinsic merits in the legislative and public bodies.
4. The organisation of the electorates.
5. The organisation of an extensive educative political campaign in support of the policy enunciated above.[49]

Jinnah's attempts to create a new party that reflected his own political beliefs eventually foundered on the rocks of Swarajist suspicion and Liberal jealousy.[50] However, the political programme he laid out for the proposed party reflects his continuing commitment to constitutional methods. His final point advocating an 'extensive educative political campaign' demonstrates his awareness of the need for grassroots support but underlines his unwillingness to make an appeal on anything but political grounds.[51] While he obviously recognized the need for broad-based support, he still required the support to be politically informed. He later reiterated the importance of informed support, indicating the priority of political parties to mobilize 'educated opinion in the country on the problem of the day.'[52]

Jinnah continued to believe in Hindu-Muslim unity. In his speech before 1926 Muslim League session, he assured his listeners 'that

if we, the two communities, can settle our differences, it will be more than half the battle for responsible government won.'[53]

REFERENCES

1. Sarojini Naidu (ed.), *Mohammad Ali Jinnah, An Ambassador of Unity; His Speeches and Writings 1912-1917* (Madras: Ganesh), 1918.
2. Larry Collins and Dominique Lapierre, *Freedom at Midnight* (Delhi: Vikas), 1976, p. 101.
3. A.K. Mazumdar, *Advent of Independence* (Bombay: Bharatiya Vidya Bhawan), 1963.
4. Prakash Almeida, *Jinnah Man of Destiny* (Delhi: Kalpaz Publications), 2001, p. 38.
5. A.M. Zaidi and Shaheda Zaidi (eds.), *The Encyclopedia of Indian National Congress*, Vol. IV, 1901-1905 (New Delhi: S. Chand & Co.), 1978, pp. 591-60.
6. *Ibid.*, Vol. V, pp. 23-174.
7. Shafi enclosure in Jinnah to Wazir Hasan, 21 May 1913, 'Hindu Muslim Unity' *All India Muslim League Records*, Vol. 15, No. 16.
8. *Quaid-e-Azam Papers*, F 47, p. 25.
9. *Ibid.*, p. 27.
10. *Ibid.*, p. 40.
11. *Ibid.*, p. 41.
12. *Hardinge to Crewe*, 20 August 1914, Hardinge Papers, Vol. 120.
13. P.C. Bamford, *Histories of Non-Cooperation and Khilafat Movements* (New Delhi: Deep and Deep), 1974, p. 138.
14. Roos Keppel to Hardinge, 5 November 1915, *Hardinge Papers*, Vol. 121.
15. *Bombay Chronicle*, 22 December 1913.
16. F. Robinson, *Separation Among Muslims* (Cambridge: Cambridge University Press), 1974.
17. Ian Bryant Wells, *Jinnah's Early Politics: Ambassador of Hindu Muslim Unity* (Delhi: Permanent Black), 2005, p. 48.
18. S. Wolpert, *Tilak and Gokhale: Revolution and Reform in the Making of Modern India* (Barkeley: University of California Press), 1961, p. 269.
19. Ian Bryant Wells, *Jinnah's Early Politics: Ambassador of Hindu Muslim Unity, op. cit.*, p. 48.
20. *Ibid.*
21. *Bombay Chronicle*, 15 January 1915.
22. *Ibid.*
23. *Ibid.*, 2 November 1915.
24. S.S. Pirzada (ed.), *The Collected Works of Quaid-e-Azam Mohammad Ali Jinnah*, Vol. I (Karachi: East West Publishing), 1969, p. 131.
25. *All India Muslim League Records*, Vol. 95, p. 46.

26. S.S. Pirzada (ed.), *Foundations of Pakistan, All India Muslim League Documents* 1906-1947 (Karachi: National Publishing House), 1969, p. 94.
27. *Bombay Chronicle*, 20 October 1915.
28. *Ibid.*, 20 November 1915.
29. *Hardinge Papers*, Vol. 90.
30. *Bombay Chronicle*, 11, December 1915.
31. S.S. Pirzada (ed.), *Foundations of Pakistan, All India Muslim League Documents* 1906-1947, *op. cit.*, pp. 351-53.
32. *Bombay Chronicle*, 30 December 1915.
33. S.S. Pirzada (ed.), *Foundations of Pakistan, All India Muslim League Documents* 1906-1947, *op. cit.*, p. 577.
34. M.R. Jayakar, *The Story of My Life* Vol. II (Bombay: Asia Publishing House), 1959, pp. 485 and 489.
35. *India Quaterly Register*, 1924, Vol. I, p. 190.
36. M.R. Jayakar, *The Story of My Life* Vol. II, *op. cit.*, p. 535.
37. D. Page, *Prelude to Pakistan* (Delhi: Oxford University Press), 1982, p. 122.
38. M.R. Jayakar, *The Story of My Life* Vol. II, *op. cit.*, p. 535.
39. *India Quaterly Register*, 1925, Vol. I, pp. 66-67.
40. S.S. Pirzada (ed.), *Foundations of Pakistan, All India Muslim League Documents* 1906-1947, *op. cit.*, p. 582.
41. *Bombay Chronicle*, 19 June 1924.
42. *Ibid.*, 17 November 1926.
43. Kidwai to Moti Lal, 5 December 1924, *AICC Papers*, 37/1925.
44. M.R. Jayakar, *The Story of My Life* Vol. II, *op. cit.*, p. 497.
45. Moti Lal, to Kidwai 8 December 1924, *AICC Papers*, 37/1925.
46. D. Page, *Prelude to Pakistan, op. cit.*, pp. 121-123.
47. M.R. Jayakar, *The Story of My Life* Vol. II, *op. cit.*, p. 559.
48. *Ibid.*
49. *Bombay Chronicle*, 4 June 1925.
50. M.R. Jayakar, T*he Story of My Life* Vol. II, *op. cit.*, p. 561.
51. *Bombay Chronicle*, 4 June 1925.
52. *Bombay Chronicle*, 10 November 1925.
53. S.S. Pirzada (ed.), *Foundations of Pakistan, All India Muslim League Documents* 1906-1947, *op. cit.*, p. 104.

3

THE FOURTEEN POINTS

In August 1928, the report of the Committee appointed by an All-Parties Conference—which had met intermittently without achieving agreement on essentials between February and May 1928—to determine the principles of the Constitution of India, was published. The Committee of nine was headed by Pandit Motilal Nehru and included two Muslim members in their individual capacity, Ali Iman and Shuaib Qureshi. However, the first did not attend most of the Committee meetings, and the second refused to sign the final draft report. The Nehru report found that separate electorates were bad for the growth of a national spirit. Weightage, which had been agreed to under the Lucknow Pact, was also disallowed: "A minority must remain a minority whether any seats are reserved for it or not." The Report rejected Iqbal's proposal for the amalgation of the Punjab, N.W.F.P., and Sind. The Report brushed aside the Muslim's fear of being dominated by the Hindu majority, and considered it 'illogical'.

An All-Parties Convention was called at Calcutta in December 1928 to consider the Nehru Report. The Muslim League, which met for its annual session at Calcutta at about the same time, appointed a strong Committee of 23 members led by Jinnah, to endeavour to bring about an adjustment of the various outstanding questions between Hindus and Musalmans arising out of the Nehru Report. With the agreement of this Committee, Jinnah suggested the following amendments in the Nehru Report to the Convention:

1. The Muslim representation in the Central Legislature should not be less than one-third.

2. In the event of adult sufferage not being granted as proposed in the Nehru Report, Muslim representation in the Punjab and Bengal Legislatures should be on a population basis, subject to re-examination after 10 years.
3. Residuary powers should be vested in the provinces and not in the Centre.
4. The separation of Sind from Bombay and the elevation of the N.W.F.P. to a Governor's Province should not be made contingent on the establishment of the Nehru Constitution.[1]

When the Convention rejected these suggestions, Jinnah's reaction was stated in one decisive sentence. "This", he said, "is the parting of the ways!"[2] It was only after the failure of this effort at reconciliation that the Muslims finally denounced the Nehru Report. In the words of Sir Azizul Huq, it was "a coffin marked three seats". An All-Parties Muslim Conference held at Delhi in January 1929, under the Chairmanship of the Aga Khan, defined the Muslim attitude. An agreement between the Jinnah and the Shafi groups was reached with the avowed purpose of re-uniting the League. It was arranged that the two wings of the League should meet simultaneously in Delhi at the end of March and pass identical resolution in favour of a joint-sitting.

By March 28, 1929, the delegates to the meeting of the two Leagues had assembled at Delhi; but as serious illness prevented Sir Mohammad Shafi's attendance, the proceedings of the proposed meeting did not go according to plan. Disagreement developed between the two groups, especially on the question of separate electorates. As a result, the followers of Sir Shafi refused to join the open session. In addition, a rowdy element appeared at the meeting evidently determined to turn the affair into a fiasco; and Jinnah was obliged to dissolve the meeting.[3]

The difficulties Jinnah faced in Indian politics at the beginning of 1929 were augmented by the humiliation he had felt at his treatment at the All Parties' Conference the previous December. The relevance of constitutional politicians, Jinnah included, with limited mass support, came increasingly under the microscope during this period. For Jinnah, the situation was exacerbated by the creation of the All India Muslim Conference in the closing months of 1928. The Muslims of the Punjab and Bengal were particularly attracted to the new organization and this prevented a reunification of the Muslim League under Jinnah. As a consequence, the Jinnah League continued to operate throughout 1929 but found it increasingly difficult to attain a quorum of members. The political relevance of Jinnah and his League diminished steadily in the early months of 1929 and it is apparent that some action was necessary to stop its complete departure from the Indian political scene. Jinnah tried to increase the relevance of his League by formulating a new set of Muslim proposals upon which a Hindu Muslim agreement might be reached. The amendments to the Nehru Report that he considered adequate in 1928 were now no longer sufficient. What was required was complete communal agreement. Apart from the benefits of an agreement between the two communities, Jinnah saw the two main objectives of his scheme as being the rejuvenation of the Muslim League and the unification of the Muslim community. In the former instance, the revival of the Muslim League also represented the revival of his own political career, while the latter he viewed as being crucial to an agreement with the Hindus. Just as he saw Hindu Muslim unity as a prerequisite to political reform for India, he now saw unity within the Muslim community as necessary to the success of negotiations with the Hindus.

The achievement of unity within the Muslim community was a daunting task. At the beginning of 1929, no one organization could claim to be the main political representative of the Muslim community. The All India Muslim Conference was emerging as a major contender for the title but there were many challengers. The Khilafat Conference was still in existence at this time, although, its president, Mohamed Ali, had joined the Jinnah camp after becoming disenchanted with the Hindu dominated Congress. The Muslim League continued to exist as a divided organization with both Shafi and Jinnah operating organizations under the title of the All India Muslim League, albeit that Shafi's League had faded somewhat, as most Punjabi and Bengali Muslim leaders were attracted to the Muslim Conference. Even within the Jinnah League itself there was significant dissension and division. To devise a scheme which would appease all the warring factions was indeed formidable.

Initially, Jinnah approached the task by attempting to remove the major cause of Muslim division from the Indian political debate. The Nehru Report had caused much dispute with both the Muslim community and his own political organization and the Muslim League's rejection of the report had led to the resignation of several of its members, including the League secretary and Jinnah's long time political follower M.C. Chagla.[4] Jinnah's tactic of treating the Nehru Report as a 'dead' issue was an attempt to defuse the controversy. On 30 March 1929, he reconvened the session of the Muslim League that had broken up in disarray in Calcutta the previous December. He again argued the case against the Nehru Report, the difference now being that he no longer called for amendments to the report, as he had done three months previously: 'The Nehru Report proposals can ... best be treated only as counter Hindu proposals to the Muslim proposals and as there is no agreement reached, it is now open for the League to take such action and adopt such course as the League think proper in the best interests of the community and the country.'[5] Jinnah advocated the formulation of a new set of Muslim proposals, comprehensive enough to attract the support of the broad spectrum of Muslim, India. In response to this need, he defined fifteen points upon which the hopes of Indian Muslims could be laid.[6] These points were eventually reduced to fourteen by Jinnah, who hoped to gain status for the proposals through comparison with the famous Fourteen Points of American President Wilson.[7] The fifteenth point was included only as a possible alternative to the preceding provision.

The Fourteen Points emerged from an intensive period of negotiations before the March 1929 Muslim League meeting.[8] During these negotiations Jinnah attempted to placate all the warring factions of the Muslim League to the extent that Mahomed Ali referred to him respectfully as the 'arch compromiser' of Indian politics.[9] However, Jinnah's attempts were unsuccessful. In the face of opposition from nationalist Muslims, including Ansari, Sherwani and Mohammad Alam, he was unable to even present his draft proposals to the Muslim League session. Ansari and his followers supported the Nehru Report as it stood and opposed any alternative scheme. On the day that Jinnah was to present his proposals, a melee erupted among members as Alam assumed the chair and Ansari attempted to force through a motion accepting the Nehru Report in its entirety.[10] Arriving late, Jinnah adjourned the meeting, returning the Muslim League to political limbo.[11] Despite this initial failure by Jinnah to gain acceptance for his fourteen points, he continued to present the scheme as a basis for political agreement between the Hindu and Muslim communities in India.

The chaos of the non-cooperation campaign, and what he saw as the growing influence of Hindu communalists in Congress during the 1920s, convinced Jinnah that protection for the Muslim community was needed at the provincial level. That protection was partly supplied by the first of Jinnah's fourteen points.

1. The form of the future Constitution should be federal with residuary powers vested in the provinces, Central Government to have control only of such matters of common interest as may be guaranteed by the Constitution.[12] By strictly controlling the powers of the central government, Jinnah hoped to allay Muslim fears of a Hindu dominated centre. The proposal also had the benefit of attracting provincial support for his plan without undermining his aims for self-government, as the provincial autonomy offered in point one in no way reduced the role of the central government. Point two was similarly aimed at provincial politicians.
2. Uniform measure of autonomy shall be granted to all provinces.[13] By advocating equity between the provinces, Jinnah was offering provincial Muslim politicians, and particularly those of the Punjab and Bengal, a further assurance that Muslim dominated provinces would not be disadvantaged under self-government.

   Points three and four of Jinnah's scheme originate from his Delhi Proposals of the previous year.
3. All legislatures in the country and other elected bodies should be reconstituted on the definite principle of

adequate and effective representation of minorities in every province without reducing the majority of any province to a minority or even equality.

4. In the Central Legislature Muslim representation should not be less than one-third.[14] Adequate representation for minorities, and in particular the Muslim community, was a linchpin of Jinnah's political strategy during the 1920s. By 1928 he believed that the level of Muslim representation needed to be guaranteed to ensure the protection of Muslim rights. The demand for 'adequate and effective representation' was also intended to gain him the support of Muslims from the minority provinces who sought political representation in excess of the percentage of Muslim people in their population.[15] Point three was also aimed specifically at Punjabis, who feared a reduction in their majority status. By encompassing the notion that a majority community within a province could not be reduced to a minority or even an equality, he actively sought Punjabi support. The latter of these two points reflects Jinnah's own political aspirations. With one-third of the representation in the Central Legislature, Jinnah felt he could hold the balance of power in any government formed, thus satisfying two aims, namely sufficient representation for the Muslim community and the opportunity to take a leading part in a self-governing India. Gandhi's rise to power had severely thwarted Jinnah's political ambitions and he eagerly sought a return to the prominence he had enjoyed prior to 1918.

   Points five and six of Jinnah's scheme were again targeted at the Muslim majority provinces of the Punjab and Bengal, whose continued separation from mainstream Muslim League politics was a particular embarrassment to Jinnah.

5. The representation of communal groups should continue to be by means of separate electorates as at present, provided that it should be open to any community at any time to abandon its separate electorate in favour of joint electorates.

6. Any territorial redistribution that might at anytime be necessary should not in anyway affect the Muslim majority in the Punjab, Bengal and the North West Frontier Province.[16]

   Separate representation was a continuing demand of both the Punjabis and the Bengalis and Jinnah recognized the need to embrace this demand to regain support from the two Muslim majority provinces. Two years previously, in the Delhi Proposals, he had offered to concede separate electorates in return for a specified list of demands, but by 1929 he was no longer in a position to make such an offer. Protection against territorial redistribution was an issue that had not previously arisen. If the Punjabis and Bengalis were aware of this possibility, they had given no indication of concern.

   Point seven was directed at both Muslims of the minority provinces and conservative Muslim opinion which had previously seen Jinnah as far too secular in his Western attire and with his Liberal social views.

7. Full religious liberty, that is, liberty of belief, worship, observances, propaganda, association and education should be guaranteed to all communities.[17] The Muslims of the United Provinces were a particular target for point seven and Jinnah hoped to benefit from the expected positive reaction to the proposal. From 1923 until 1925 the United Provinces was the centre of violence between Hindus and Muslims and, after a year of relative calm,[18] 1927 had been another year of bloodshed. There were many reasons for this continued violence. D. Page identifies the Arya Samaj's *shuddhi* campaign against the Malkana Rajputs of Agra in 1923 as the beginning of violence in the United Provinces.[19] Regardless of its origins, violence soon took on a communal character and Jinnah proposed religious protection was welcomed by the influential United Provinces' Muslims. Education was also emerging as a major concern in some of the Muslim minority provinces, particularly the United Provinces,

where Muslims were increasingly concerned with a Hindu dominated legislature. This was an area consistently pursued by Jinnah throughout his political career.

Within point eight of his scheme, Jinnah included the concept of a communal veto.

8. No Bill or Resolution, or any part thereof, should be passed in any legislative or any other elected body, if three-fourths of the members of any community in that particular body oppose such a Bill or Resolution or part thereof, on the ground that it would be injurious to the interests of that community or, in the alternative, such other method is devised as may be found feasible and practicable to deal with such cases.[20]

The notion of a veto by three quarters of any community was first raised in 1916 and incorporated in the Lucknow Pact. In 1927, in response to the Delhi Proposals, the Congress again offered the right of veto to the Muslims.[21] By including this in his scheme, Jinnah recognized the communal veto as advantageous to his community. Further, he knew that it would be difficult for the Congress to reject such a proposal after earlier supporting it. When the veto was initially put forward during the Lucknow Pact negotiations, it had been to placate the United Provinces Muslims in their demands for greater representation. Jinnah's re-introduction of the same proposal again attracted him support from the same source.

Points nine and ten complete those taken from the Delhi Proposals of 1927.

9. Sindh should be separated from the Bombay Presidency.

10. Reforms should be introduced in the North West Frontier Province and Baluchistan on the same footing as in other provinces.[22] Jinnah saw the creation of the North West Frontier Province and Baluchistan as separate province and the separation of Sindh from Bombay as a major benefit to both his political aspirations and those of Muslim India. The creation of three new Muslim majority

provinces would put him in a stronger position in regard to both the Congress and the government. The existence of Hindu minorities in almost half the provinces greatly enhanced the Muslim position in Hindu dominated provinces. The domination of Muslim politics by the Punjabis and Bengalis would also be severely undermined by the presence of three new Muslim provinces. In the light of his recent difficulties, Jinnah saw this latter fact as particularly important.

In point eleven Jinnah again aimed to gain the support of conservative provincial opinion.

11. Provision should be made in the Constitution giving the Muslims an adequate share along with other Indians in all the Services of the State and in self-governing bodies, having due regard to the requirements of efficiency.[23] Early in his Political career Jinnah had indicated his reluctance to support the reservation of a percentage of positions in the bureaucracy for any Indians, preferring that positions go to the best qualified applicants.[24] The inclusion of this demand reflects his change of circumstance in the previous decade. Provincial Muslim opinion was in favour of a specified percentage of the civil service and other government bodies being set aside for the Muslim community. Jinnah hoped to channel this opinion into support for his scheme and consequently for him personally.

In point twelve Jinnah clarified the issues he had already raised in point seven.

12. The Constitution should embody 'adequate safeguards for the protection of Muslim religion, culture and personal law and the promotion of Muslim education, language, religion, personal laws, Muslim charitable institutions, and for their due share in grants in aid given by the State and by self-governing bodies.'[25] Although Jinnah was reiterating what was said previously, Islam is specified as being in need of protection. Also listed are specific issues which concerned the Muslim community at large,

notably the issues of language and education. Education was a thorny question in some minority provinces, especially the United Provinces. The continuation of Urdu as an official language was similarly jealously protected by Muslims of this same province. While this point was clearly aimed at gaining support for Jinnah from conservative Muslim leaders as well as dissipating his secular image, the appeal was consistent with his continuing liberal view of politics.

In point thirteen of his scheme Jinnah again mixed his own political ambitions with those whose support he sought.

13. No Cabinet, either Central or Provincial, should be formed without there being a proportion of Muslim Ministers at least one-third of the numbers *appointed*.[26] Jinnah wanted one-third Muslim membership of the central cabinet but was not committed to the concept at the provincial level. Muslim leaders in the minority provinces were, however, greatly attracted to the notion and he hoped to tap this support by including it in his proposals. Point fourteen of the draft proposals was another designed as a protective measure for the Muslim community.

14. No change to be made in the Constitution by the Central Legislature except with the concurrence of the States constituting the Indian Federation.'[27] The specification that all constitutional changes needed the agreement of all states ensured the continuation of minority protection. The final point of the proposals was eventually included only as an alternative to point fourteen. In this point, Jinnah confirmed the principle of separate representation that he had put forward in point five, but here dealt specifically with the Muslim community. That in the present circumstances the representation of Musalmans in the different legislatures of this country and of the other elected bodies through separate electorates is inevitable, and, further, Government being pledged not to deprive the Musalmans of this right, it cannot be taken away without their consent, and so long as the Musalmans are

> not satisfied that their rights and interest are safeguarded in the manner specified above (or herein) they would in no way consent to the establishment of joint electorates with or without conditions.[28]

By confirming his commitment to the continuation of communal representation, Jinnah answered Muslim critics concerned over his willingness to concede them in 1927.

To a large degree, Jinnah's acquiescence in many of the demands found within his scheme can be recognized as a deliberate attempt to gain wide support within the Muslim community. A query remains as to whether the Fourteen Points were a legitimate attempt to establish a viable negotiating position with the Hindu community or whether, as argued by Motilal Nehru, Jinnah 'was simply trying to reinstate himself with his followers by making preposterous demands'.[29] An argument can certainly be presented to show that Motilal is correct. There were aspects of the Fourteen Points which were unacceptable to the Hindu community, raising questions about the scheme's viability. Specifically point thirteen, calling for a one-third representation of Muslims in cabinets at both the central and provincial levels, was both outside the scope of Jinnah's own political ambitions and unacceptable to the Hindu community. It would be unrealistic for Jinnah to have believed that the Hindus would concede such a demand. The demand did relate directly to the aspirations of the Muslims of some of the minority provinces and particularly the Muslims of the United Provinces, who had demanded one-third representation for their community as early as 1916. However, Motilal's assessment does not fully analyse Jinnah's motives. Jinnah quite often operated on a number of levels politically, and while he desired to unite the Muslim community, he did not wish to do so at the cost of Hindu Muslim unity. The Fourteen Points can more accurately be seen as a stick to encourage Congress to grant Jinnah's more conservative political goals. The document contained several demands not especially important to Jinnah, which he could concede to the Hindus without damaging his support base in the Muslim community. For example, he would have been able to concede one-third representation in the cabinets of those provinces where Muslim minorities were limited in number or influence.[30]

The Fourteen Points advocated by Jinnah received a lukewarm reception from the Muslim community and were only elevated in status when Jinnah's star began to rise again in the late 1930s. Consequently, his position as a representative of the Muslim community remained uncertain to the end of the 1920s. Only a few close friends and Legislative Assembly colleagues welcomed his scheme, with the majority of these Muslim politicians also having limited support in the community. Among the Hindus, the Fourteen Points were scorned, with Jawaharlal Nehru referring to them as 'Jinnah's ridiculous 14 points'[31]. In 1929 Jawaharlal was president of the Congress and his ongoing hostility towards Jinnah was reflective of the attitude of younger Congressmen. After his initial failure to unite the Muslim community, Jinnah again turned to the role of a mediator. On this occasion, however, he aimed his approaches at the viceregal level, attempting to win concessions from the administration and carry political India with him after achieving success.

REFERENCES

1. S.S. Pirzada (ed.), *Foundations of Pakistan: All-India Muslim League Documents,* Vol. I (New Delhi: Metropolitan Books), 1982, p. lxiii.
2. Hector Bolitho, *Jinnah, Creator of Pakistan* (London: John Murray), 1954, p. 95.
3. Waheed-uz-Zaman, *Towards Pakistan* (Lahore: Publishers United Lt.), 1954, p. 58.
4. *Bombay Chronicle,* 29 November 1928.
5. M.A. Jinnah, *History of the Origin of Fourteen Points* (Bombay: n.d). (Australia: Flinders University).
6. *Quaid-e-Azam Papers*, pp. 1-3.
7. Durga Das, *India from Curzon to Nehru and After* (New York: John Doby), 1970.
8. S. S. Hasan, Plain Mr. Jinnah: Selections from Quaid-e-Azam correspondence relating mainly to personal matters (Karachi: Royal Book Company), 1976, pp. 47-48.
9. *Ibid.*
10. *Ibid.*

11. *Ibid.*
12. M.A. Jinnah, *History of the Origin of Fourteen Points, op. cit.*
13. *Ibid.*
14. *Ibid.*
15. *Ibid.*
16. *Ibid.*
17. *Ibid.*
18. Ian Bryant Wells, *Jinnah's Early Politics: Ambassador of Hindu Muslim Unity* (Delhi: Permanent Black), 2005, p. 190.
19. D. Page, *Prelude to Partition* (Delhi: Oxford University Press), 1982, p. 74.
20. M.A. Jinnah, *History of the Origin of Fourteen Points, op. cit.*
21. Ian Bryant Wells, *Jinnah's Early Politics: Ambassador of Hindu Muslim Unity, op. cit.*, p.190.
22. M. A. Jinnah, *History of the Origin of Fourteen Points, op. cit.*
23. *Ibid.*
24. S.S. Pirzada (ed.) *The Collected Works of Quaid-e-Azam Mohammad Ali Jinnah,* Vol. I (Karachi: East West Publishing), 1984, pp. 229-30.
25. M.A. Jinnah, *History of the Origin of Fourteen Points, op. cit.*
26. *Ibid.*
27. *Ibid.*
28. *Ibid.*
29. D. Page, *Prelude to Partition* (Delhi: Oxford University Press), 1982, p. 200.
30. Ian Bryant Wells, Jinnah's *Early Politics: Ambassador of Hindu Muslim Unity, op. cit.*, p.194.
31. *Ibid.*

4

THE MUSLIM LEAGUE

It was on 1 October, 1906 that a delegation of about seventy Muslims led by the Aga Khan was received in the ballroom of the Viceroy's house at Simla by Lord Minto. The delegation had brought with it an address signed by nobles, ministers of various states, great landowners, lawyers, merchants, and of many other of His Majesty's Mahommedan subjects'. They asked for separate representation of Muslims in all levels of government—District Boards, Municipalities, and Legislative Councils. They drew the attention of the Viceroy to the fact that in the United Provinces, where Muslims constituted fourteen per cent of the population, they had not secured a single seat by joint franchise.[1] And if by chance they were to win any seats, Muslim candidates would have to pander to the 'views of the Hindu majority and thus go against the interests of their own community'. Lord Minto assured the delegation that he was entirely in accord with their case. Muslims had won separate representation for themselves.[2]

A fierce controversy has raged in India ever since the time that this concession was granted to Muslims. Maulana Muhammad Ali is reported to have characterized the delegation as a command performance, though it is well known that later he put forward the view that separate electorates diminished communal bitterness.[3] Rajendra Prasad has taken great pains to prove that the delegation was engineered by Archhold, the British Principal of Aligarh College.[4] This was quite understandable. Sir Sayyid had tried to promote understanding between Muslims and the British Government and Archhold was, after all, a Principal of a Muslim college. Like his predecessors, he was extremely well-disposed towards Muslim interests. To show that the delegation was engineered by the British Government or officials is probably to suggest that Muslims were being supported by the British. This was quite true. But so was the establishment of the Indian National Congress largely inspired by British influence. And no less a person than the British Viceroy, Lord Dufferin, was behind the idea of the Congress being established on political lines, rather than it restricting its activities to purely social reforms. The latter was the idea of A.O. Hume, the founder of the Indian National Congress and a former Home Secretary of the Government of India. It was because of Lord Dufferin's influence that he abandoned it.[5] When Lord Dufferin was encouraging the formation of the Indian National Congress, he knew that the Congress would largely be a Hindu organization for after Muslims were nowhere in the political picture at that time. Thus, if the British could encourage the formation of a predominantly Hindu organization, why could they not help the Muslims to embark on a similar political career?

Probably, where the Nationalists' case against British concession of separate electorates to the Muslims was at its strongest was that it was a deliberate attempt to sow the seeds of conflict between Hindus and Muslims. A British official is reported to have remarked at the time the Viceroy assured the Muslim delegation that they would get separate electorates, "It is nothing less than pulling back of sixty two millions of people from joining the ranks of the seditious opposition."[6] In order to establish this charge conclusively, one would have to prove two things. First, that the British foresaw the political development of India on parliamentary lines whereby there would come into being in course of time a homogeneous electorate, mature enough to elect a government from two or three political parties. Secondly, that the British, having foreseen all this, were indulging in dividing the electorate in order to postpone for as long as possible the transfer of political power. But all the evidence goes to suggest that the British Government at that time was firmly convinced that British parliamentary institutions could not be transplanted in India. And what was more, they did not regard India as a homogeneous nation, but a sub-continent inhabited by a number of nations. Lord Morley wrote to Lord Minto: "Not one whit more than you do I think it desirable or possible, or even conceivable, to adapt English political institutions to the nations who inhabit India."[7]

In December 1906, Nawab Salimullah's scheme for the formation of the Muslim All India Confedracy, became the basis of discussion among the Muslim leaders who had assembled from all parts of India to attend the All India Mohammedan Education Conference at Dacca. Sir Rafiuddin Ahmad, one of the delegates present, recalled: "His scheme was not adopted in its entirety as the phraseology of parts of the document did not seem quite happy to the majority of the delegates, and the term confederacy grated on the ears of not a few. The spirit of the Nawab's scheme was, however, adopted and the essence approved. Therefore the object, the establishment of a central political organization for Muslims, was achieved."[8] Eventually, a public meeting of the Muslim leaders was held on December 30, 1906. Viqar ul Mulk presided. On the motion of Nawab Salimullah, it was decided that a political association be formed styled All India Muslim League, for the furtherance of the following objects:

(a) to promote among the Musalmans of India, feelings of loyalty to the British Government, and to remove any misconception that may arise as to the intention of the Government with regard to any of its measures;

(b) to protect and advance the political rights and Interests of the Musalmans of India, and to respectfully represent their needs and aspirations to the Government;

(c) to prevent the rise, among the Musalmans of India, of any feeling of hostility towards other communities, without prejudice to the other aforementioned objects of the League.[9]

The establishment of the Muslim League evoked mixed feelings in the Indian Press. The Englishman thought it would provide an effective answer to the Congress, as well as afford an avenue for the publication of Mohammedan aspirations, and remarked that "it is high time that the Mohammedans of India found a voice". *The Times of India* and *The Daily Telegraph* of Lucknow welcomed its formation. The Bengalee attacked the League and its organizers, and predicted that "it will, if it seeks to fulfil its mission, fraternize with the Congress, and eventually coalesce with it. If not, it will go the way of the Patriotic Association of the late Sir Syed Ahmad."[16]

Only a section of the British Press noticed the birth of the Muslim League. *The Times* welcomed the change, not so much as a mark of Muslim progress or unity, but as an inevitable outcome of the Congress movement, and as an exposure of the hollowness of the pretensions of Congress to speak for all of India. It reminded the more cautious agitators that agitation was a game that provoked counter agitation, and that the counter agitation might be conducted by the most warlike races of the Peninsula. Despite the pacific language of its founders, *The Times* doubted if the League's establishment would make for peace. *The Spectator*, while admitting that the objects of the League were excellent, did not like the "feeling among Muslims that they must organize in a camp by themselves. That is the real danger of the National Congress, as we have already pointed out that in agitating for union it makes for racial disunion."[11] *The Morning Post* warned the League to remain "entirely defensive and protective", and any deviation from its path "will call at once for the most drastic intervention of the British rulers." *The Contemporary Review* accorded a warm welcome to the League, analysed its aims and objects, and contrasted its constitutional and loyal approach with the Congress policy of violence. The founding of the League was ascribed to the Muslim conviction after the agitators' successful attempt at the removal of Sir Bamfylde Fuller that only by agitation could the Government be reached. "The Rubicon has been crossed", it declared, "the Muslims of India have forsaken the shades of retirement for the political arena; henceforth a new factor in Indian politics has to be reckoned with."[12]

Lord Ronaldshay believes that the birth of the Muslim League was the result of a simple but vital problem: how was a system of government which predicated homogeniety of population to be adjusted to meet the case of a population whose outstanding characteristic was its heterogeneity.[13] Percival Spear is of the opinion that the League was founded in response to the Hindu agitation against the partition of Bengal, and that since then the vitality of Muslim separatism was in direct proportion to the militancy of Hinduism.[14] K.K. Aziz feels that the Muslim League is the child of four factors: First, the old belief uttered by Sir Syed Ahmad Khan that the Muslims were somehow a separate entity; secondly, the Hindu character of the Indian National Congress, which did not allow the Muslims to associate themselves with other Indians; thirdly, the agitation against the partition of Bengal, which suggested Hindu designs of domination over Muslims; and finally, the Muslim desire to have their own exclusive electorates for all representative institutions.[15] According to B.B. Majumdar, had the plan of Syed Ameer Ali and the Central Mohammedan Association to convene the Conference of All India Muslim leaders matured in 1877, the history of the Muslim League would have been anticipated twenty years earlier.[16] M.S. Jain describes the League as a child of the Aligarh Movement. "If one looks at the activities of Sir Syed's Defence Association during 1894-96, we would find that it was the true predecessor of the Muslim League, and it asked in 1896 what the Simla Deputation asked for in 1906. The Muslim League had been founded in accordance with Sir Syed's scheme of a separate Muslim existence.[17]

Separate electorates were given constitutional recognition in the Indian Councils Act of 1909. Muslims were accorded not only the right to elect their representatives by separate electorates, but also the right to vote in the general constituencies. In addition, they were also given weightage in representation. In spite of these concessions, one could see how politically weak they were in the composition of Legislative Councils under the Act of 1909. In Bengal, where they were in a majority, there were only five Muslim representatives out of twenty eight elected members. In the United Provinces, where they were in a minority, but where their position was politically stronger than it was in Bengal, they had four representatives out of twenty one elected members. The great irony was Punjab where Muslims were supposed to be in a majority and therefore not given any special protection under the Act. There were eight elected members out of whom there was not a single Muslim.[18]

What was significant was that it was becoming increasingly apparent that Sir Sayyid had been much too over cautious in advising the Muslims to stay aloof from political activities. W. S. Blunt, who had visited India, and besides being a friend of the Muslims, was also politically shrewd, had advised Muslims on occasions in 1883-84 that they should show their teeth in order to be feared and respected by the British.

"I told them, if the Mohammedans only knew their power they would not be neglected and ill treated by the Government as they now were. In England, we were perpetually scared at the idea of a Mohammedan rising in India, and any word uttered by a Mohammedan was paid more attention to than that of twenty Hindus. But, if they sat still, thanking Providence for the favours which were denied them, the English public would be only too happy to leave them as they were."[19]

When, in the Delhi Durbar of December 1911, it was announced in the name of the King Emperor that the partition of Bengal would be annulled, it became clear to the Muslims that the British Government, pressured by Hindu agitation, would not even leave the Muslim community 'as they were'. Disestablishment of the province of East Bengal meant that the Muslims would lose their strong majority position and be once again dominated by the more advanced Hindu community.[20]

Lord Minto spoke of the repeated assurances that had been given to Muslims regarding the inviolability of partition in his speech in the House of Lords in February 1912: "We told the Musalmans that the Partition was a settled fact and we over and over again asserted that it must continue to be so. We assured the Musalman population of Eastern Bengal of our appreciation of their loyalty and our determination to safeguard their interests. I should think there could have been scarcely a Civil Servant in India who had not declared that it would be impossible for the British Government to reverse the decision it had come to as regards the maintenance of the Partition of Bengal."[21]

A bitter jest which became popular among the Muslims of Delhi was 'no bombs, no boons'.[22] The years following the abolition of partition of Bengal were a turning point in the history of Indian

Muslims. They began to wonder whether they had gone too far in both profession and practice of loyalty to the British Government. But, instead of coolly examining their position and future prospects, they tried to swing from one extreme to the other from cooperation with the British to an emotional cooperation with the Hindus. Muslim suspicions, aroused by the revocation of partition of Bengal, were further strengthened after the outbreak of the First World War when they found that the British Government was fighting against Turkey, which was the leading Muslim power. As early as 1913, the Muslim League formally adopted the Congress objective of self-government for India within the Empire. The culminating point was the Congress-League Lucknow Pact of 1916.

There is no denying the fact that no Muslim leader in the modern history of India has excelled Sir Sayyid in the great services that he rendered to his people. Other men have written books and founded colleges; but to arrest as with a wall the degeneration of a whole people, that is the work of the prophet.[23] But in trying to build Aligarh Muslim College on the lines of an English university and in imparting an unadulterated English education to Muslim students, he not only made them less fanatical but also less sincere Muslims. W.S. Blunt, an admirer of Sir Sayyid, wrote: "I myself feel rather constrained with them, for one does not know whether to treat them as pious Mohammedans, or latter day disciples of Jowett. Not that they are not extremely amiable, but there is a tone of apology in their talk to me, as much as to say 'we are not such infidels as you suppose'."[24]

But no one can better the satire on Sir Sayyid by Nazir Ahmad in his Ibn ul Waqt (The Opportunist) where the difficulties of a Muslim who was eager to adopt Western ways of living were vividly described. No translation can convey the subtlety with which Nazir Ahmad portrayed the characteristics of such a man and the qualms and contradictions that his conscience was plagued with. Nazir Ahmad pointed out that many Muslims who found the requirements of their religion too rigorous to follow welcomed such a leader.[25]

It was obvious that Western education, accompanied by imitation of Western culture, brought in its wake intellectual and cultural separation between the Muslim elite who were Westernized and loyal to the British Government, and the poorer classes of illiterate Muslims. Thus, according to Lady Minto's diary of 1910: "Aga Khan arrived to stay with us today. He seems to have had a triumphal progress through India amongst the Moslems. He says that the only real way to appeal to the feelings of Natives is by means of the superstitions of their religion, and consequently he has instructed the priests in every mosque to issue a decree that any Mohammedans who incite to rebellion, or go about preaching sedition, will be eternally damned."[26]

Western education created a chasm between Westernized Muslim leaders and those who were steeped in Islamic theology and thought. Muslim society thus came to be led by two rival groups of leaders: orthodox religious leaders, who were mostly ignorant of modern sciences and technology, and the modern educated classes who lacked Islamic fervour and had only a nodding acquaintance with their religion. Sir Sayyid was quite right when he suggested that religious reformation was essential. But who could undertake this task and build a bridge between Islamic traditions and Western sciences? Neither of the two groups of leaders was qualified to undertake such a task.

There are many people both in India and Pakistan who tend to dismiss the contribution of the Muslim League towards the achievement of Pakistan as one of little consequence. They often quote, out of context, the statement of Jinnah that his entire equipment was confined to an attache case, a typewriter, and a personal assistant.[27] It is obvious that such glib statements lack both reflection and historical perspective. Jinnah, with all his adroitness, needed an organization like the Muslim League to impress upon the British and the Congress that he enjoyed universal Muslim support. He also needed the Muslim League for winning elections. In fact the Muslim League bridged the gulf that yawned between the illiterate Muslim masses and the highly Westernized Muslims elite at the top.

What was the state of the Muslim League before Jinnah undertook its reorganization? In 1927, the total membership of the Muslim League was 1,330[28]. During the years 1931-33, its annual expenditure did not exceed Rs. 3,000.29. In the 1930 Allahabad session, when Sir Muhammad Iqbal presented his historic address demanding the establishment of a North-Western Muslim state in India, the League meeting did not even have its quorum of 75 members. Hafiz Jalandhari was asked to read his famous poem, *Shahnama-i-Islam,* to keep those who were present entertained while the organizers were busy enrolling new members in the town.[30] During this time, the annual sessions of the Muslim League were often held in private houses. The annual session of 1931, held at Delhi, was described as 'a languid and attenuated House of scarcely 120 people in all.'[31] During this session the annual subscription was reduced from Rs. 6 to Re. 1 and the admission fee of Rs. 5 was abolished to attract new members.[32] The League's declining strength was also reflected in the resolution which reduced the quorum at the annual sessions from 75 to 50.

When Jinnah started reorganizing the Muslim League in early 1935, Sir Fazl i Husain had retired from the Executive Council and returned to the Punjab to resuscitate the Unionist Party. Jinnah, who had been elected President for three years, very shrewdly invited Fazl i Husain to preside over the annual session of the Muslim League. Fazl i Husain declined the request and made it clear to Jinnah that he should desist from setting up a Central Parliamentary Board of the Muslim League because Muslims in Provinces like the Punjab might like to work with non-communal organizations in which case a Central Muslim Parliamentary Board would hamper their efforts in creating communal harmony. Fazl i Husain, writing to Sikander Hyat, said, "I have also asked Ahmad Yar (Daultana's father) to strongly press on him (Jinnah) the advisability of keeping his finger out of the Punjab pie."[33] Jinnah did not make any headway in the Punjab, even though he was reported to have made promises of procuring large election funds from Bombay millionaires and the Raja of Mahmoodabad. At that time, the prospects of Jinnah's success were so dim that even a former founder of the Muslim League like the Aga Khan lent his financial support to the Unionist Party.[34] The weakness of the League was reflected in the elections of 1937 when it won only 4.6 per cent of the total Muslim votes.

But in April 1938, Jinnah was claiming that during the last six months the Muslim League had enrolled members by hundreds of thousands.[35] Even though the Congress had launched its Muslim mass contact movement by January 1938 it could claim the support of only a hundred thousand (or 33 per cent) Muslims out of its 3.1 million members.[36] Thus, the great majority of politically conscious Muslims were joining the Muslim League. In 1944, the Muslim League officially claimed a membership of some two millions.[37] Its organization had penetrated the country-side and those Muslims who openly remained hostile to the Muslim League were not considered Muslims by their co religionists. By the end of 1944, the Bengal Muslim League claimed a membership of about half a million and the Sind and Panjab Leagues had 200,000 members each. But the most convincing testimony of the Muslim League's strength came from the 1945-46 election results. The Muslim League polled about 4.5 million or 75 per cent of the Muslim votes in the elections.[38] It won 460 out of the 533 Muslim seats in the Central and Provincial elections.

The question arises that if the organization and power of the Muslim League were entirely due to the drive and organizing ability of Jinnah, why was it that the Muslim League prior to the thirties, when Jinnah was one of its leading figures, was a dormant body? Jinnah had been President of the, Muslim League during the years 1919-30. The Secretary of the League, lamenting Jinnah's decision to leave the country in 1931, said in his annual report: "Mr. M.A. Jinnah had been the life and the moving spirit of the League for many years and the success of the institution during the last 9 years was due to his earnestness, devotion and statesmanship."[39] Did the Muslim League receive new impetus first as a result of the shortsightedness of the Congress in excluding Muslim League representatives from the Provincial Congress Cabinets in 1937 and later owing to the alleged persecutions that the Muslims suffered during the regimes of 1937-39 Choudhry Khaliquzzaman seem to think that the former was the main cause which helped the League to rally the Muslims under its banner[40]. There is no doubt that this did help the League. But how was it that the Muslim League did not achieve its maximum strength during these years of alleged Congress persecutions? It was only after the Lahore Resolution was passed and the demand for a separate Muslim State came to the forefront that Muslims in their thousands flocked to the Muslim

League. Thus, neither Jinnah's organizing ability nor the alleged Congress misrule by themselves could have transformed the League into a mighty force. The demand for Pakistan reminded Muslims of their past glory and opened before them vast and fascinating vistas of future greatness. It was this stimulant which put life and vigour into the Muslim League.

Those who think that Pakistan was entirely a product of Hindu hostility to Muslims not only exaggerate Hindu responsibility for it but also forget that Muslims were just as hostile. In addition to all this, they have not appreciated the demand for Pakistan in its historical perspective. Muslims had ruled India and they could not understand why under a democratic system they should be deprived of power and influence. Thus, it was this desire for power and unwillingness to live under those whom they had governed which largely explains the demand for Pakistan. Jinnah was groping towards this even before the demand for Pakistan was launched.

"Muslims have made it clear more than once that besides the question of religion, culture, language and personal laws, there is another question of life and death for them and that their future destiny and fate are dependent upon their securing their political rights, their due share in the national life, the Government and the administration of the country."[41]

Muslim educated classes were not so much concerned about their religious and cultural rights as they were about their share in the government of the country. The tremendous following that Jinnah had among these classes lay in the fact that he offered to them political power under a new Muslim State. "Which government claiming to be a civilized government can demolish our mosque, or which government is going to interfere with religion which is strictly a matter between God and man? The question is that Musalmans are a nation distinct from the Hindu. It is a historical fact that the Musalmans are a separate nation and hence we must have our own States."[42]

But a great majority of the two anna members of the Muslim League were not westernized educated Muslims. They were simple rural folk or the poorer sections of the urban Muslims who were told time and again by their mullahs that power would be given to them by God if they became good Muslims. Thus, the idea of establishing a Muslim State was not new. Less sophisticated and anti-League Muslim organizations like the Ahrar and the Khaksar had talked about it. The Ahrars forward the idea of Hakumat i Ilahla (Government of God) and the Khaksars claim that their aim was Istikhlaf al-Ard [Establishment of Khilafat (Islamic Government) on earth].[43] Thus, when the League demanded Pakistan, it was responding to this inner urge for political power among the Muslims. The Muslim League was, on one hand satisfying a craving for power and influence free from Hindu competition among the Muslim intelligentsia and, on the other, the more vague and religious urge for power among the Muslim masses. The League, in this sense, had become a more comprehensive and representative organization than the Khilafat movement which did not attract the full support of Westernized and educated Muslims.

The Muslim League, like the Congress, was not a political party in the ordinary sense of the term. It was a national movement whose aim was the establishment of separate sovereign State of Pakistan. Any man who stood against the League was called a traitor or quisling by the Quaid-e-Azam. Some of the Muslim Leaguers went so far as to say that any Muslim who opposed the Muslim League had betrayed the cause of Islam itself. As long as Pakistan remained unachieved, all Muslims were supposed to subordinate their personal and ideological difference to the national goal.

"We shall have time to quarrel ourselves and we shall have time when these differences will have to be settled, when wrongs and injuries will have to be remedied. We shall have time for domestic programme and policies, but first get the Government. This is a nation without any territory or any government."[44]

Thus, within the Muslim League could be found feudal land owners, industrialists, the ulema, the lower middle classes, industrial workers and peasants. In it were socialists like Mian Iftikharuddin and extreme leftist elements like Danyal Latifi, who had joined the League after it had become clear that the goal Pakistan was within sight. The leadership of Jinnah and the organization and discipline of the Muslim League were such that all these heterogeneous elements could be kept within the League without impairing its unity. Similarly, the passionate zeal for Pakistan was such that Bengalis and Punjabis, though conscious of their differences, were willing to work together for the common goal.

Jinnah very cleverly kept himself and the League scrupulously out of all controversial issues. He himself was a Shiah and a Khoja by origin, but always said that he was only a Muslim and also offered his public prayers with the Sunni Muslims. The simple doctrine that he preached was that Islam transcended all petty sectarian differences. Since there was no state, no debates about what form of Islam should be established or practiced could arise. And the sort of Islam that the Muslim League put forward was simple and straightforward, free of all theological and doctrinal subtleties, which the ordinary Muslim masses could understand. This intellectual naivete was such that it pervaded not only the Muslim masses but infected the leaders as well.

The growth of the Muslim League was also helped considerably by the total absence of any competition from other political parties, particularly after 1942 when the Congress leaders were in jail. Jinnah himself frankly admitted that he shuddered when he considered what was going to happen in 1939. 'There was going to be a deal between Mr. Gandhi and Lord Linlithgow. Providence helped us. The war which nobody welcomes proved to be a blessing in disguise'. On the other hand, it could also be argued that the Congress-Muslim mass contact movement had not proved successful earlier and was not likely to produce any different results if tried later. Moreover, if the Congress had remained in power, there might have arisen differences between the Congress High Command and the Provincial Ministries or between leaders in the High Command itself like Nehru and Patel. Congressmen, by going to jail and taking a stand against the British Government, created for themselves such support and sympathy that even the Communists, who tried to infiltrate into every segment of Indian political life, could not make much head-way.

The Congress Party has been criticized for its Unitarian structure and the way it nullified Provincial autonomy controlling the Provincial Governments.[46] Sometimes Gandhi's interference in

Congress affairs and his comparisons of the Congress structure with that of an army so created the impression that the Congress was imitating Fascist methods.[47] Jinnah was also quick to detect such Fascist features in the Congress organisation. But he has also been subjected to the same sort of criticism in the sense that when the League organization became powerful, he saw to it that the Muslim League Provincial Parliamentary Parties and Governments carried out the instructions issued to them from the Centre. He was also sometimes fond of comparing the Muslim League with an army with himself as the general. Thus, he talked of giving marching orders when the Muslims were disciplined and ready.[48] When his mission of achieving Pakistan was accomplished in June 1947, he was reported to have said: 'I have done my job. When the Field Marshal leads his army into victory, it is for the civil authority to take over.'[49]

When Jinnah started reorganizing the Muslim League during 1935-37, he proceeded very cautiously and wanted to enlist as much support as possible of the influential Muslim leaders. He invited Sir Fazl i Husain to preside over the annual session of the Muslim League in 1935. In the Lucknow session in 1937, the Muslim League acquired tremendous strength when Fazl ul Huq, the Premier of Bengal, and Sir Sikander Hyat Khan, the Premier of Punjab, declared their support for the Muslim League and brought over their parties to the Muslim League ranks. At that time, Jinnah's main concern was to build the Muslim League as a powerful and well organized party and the power he enjoyed depended very much upon the support that he obtained from powerful Muslim groups in various Provinces.

It was in 1941 that one got the impression for the first time that the power of the President was not only dependent upon the League as a party but had also acquired a personal character. The Quaid-e-Azam had emerged.[50] One cannot help admiring the strategy that Jinnah followed in building up his power and prestige as the League President. In July 1941, the Viceroy announced that the Premiers of the Punjab, Bengal, Assam and Sind had been invited to join the National Defence Council. The Muslim League had been following a very shrewd and cautious policy whereby it neither cooperated whole heartedly with the British war effort nor did it take any steps to obstruct it. But it certainly did not want to create the impression that, unlike the Congress, it lacked national fervour for the freedom of the country. When the invitations to the Provincial Premiers to join the National Defence Council were issued, Jinnah knew that the Viceroy had made a tactical mistake by inviting them as representatives of the Muslim community. The Premiers of the Punjab, Bengal and Assam were under the impression that they had been invited to represent their Provinces and indicated their willingness to join the National Defence Council. (At that time Sind did not have a Muslim League Ministry.) When Jinnah issued peremptory orders to them to resign from the National Defence Council, they were resentful. But when he confronted Sir Sikander Hyat, the Premier of Punjab, with the text of the message that the Viceroy had sent to him through the Governor of Bombay, Sir Sikander Hyat had no choice except to tender his resignation from the National Defence Council because the message indicated that he had been invited as a representative of the Muslim community.[51] This was followed by the resignation of Sir Saadullah, the Premier of Assam. Fazl ul Huq at first was extremely resentful and reluctant, but later he had to resign as well. He complained that Jinnah had known of their selection at least a day before the names were published but did not care to indicate his disapproval immediately. "He kept waiting and watching till our names were published and then he came out with his thunder that he had decided to take disciplinary action against us. He took us unawares as if he was anxious to make a public exhibition of his authority."[52] Similarly, Begum Shah Nawaz, who had joined the National Defence Council, was called upon to resign but when she refused, she was expelled from the Muslim League for five years. This was followed by the expulsion of Sir Sultan Ahmad for having joined the Viceroy's Executive Council contrary to the decision of the Muslim League and its general policy. This 'exhibition of authority' made the Muslims realize how powerful their Quaid-e-Azam was in the sense that powerful Muslim leaders could not easily flout his instructions without incurring the wrath of Muslim public opinion.

REFERENCES

1. H.G. Rawlinson, *The British Achievements in India* (London: William Hodge), 1948, p. 188.
2. Mary Countess of Minto, *India Minto and Morley* 1905-910 (London: Macmillan), 1934, p. 47.
3. Afzal Iqbal (ed.), *Select Writings and Speeches of Maulana Mohamed Ali* (Lahore: Ashsaf), 1944, p. 255.
4. Rajendra Prasad, *India Divided* (Bombay: Kitabs), 1947, pp. 112-113.
5. B. Pattabhi Sitaramayya, *The History of Indian National Congress,* Vol. I, 1985-1935 (Bombay: Padma Publications), 1946, p. 15.
6. Mary Countess of Minto, *India Minto and Morley* 1905-910, *op. cit.*, pp. 47-49.
7. John Viscount Morley, *Recollections,* Vol. II (London: Macmillan), 1918, p. 172.
8. S.S. Pirzada (ed.), *Foundations of Pakistan,* All-India Muslim League Documents 1906-1947, Vol. I (New Delhi: Metropolitan Book Co.), 1982, p. 1.
9. *Ibid.*
10. *Ibid.*
11. *Ibid.*
12. *Ibid.*
13. *Ibid.*
14. Percival Spear, *India Pakistan and the West* (London: Oxford University Press), 1958, p. 207.
15. K.K. Aziz, *The Making of Pakistan* (London: Chatto & Windus), 1967, p. 29.
16. B.B. Majumdar, *Indian Political Association and Reforms of Legislatures* (1818-1917) (Calcutta: Minerva), 1945, p. 227.
17. M.S. Jain, *The Aligarh Movement: Its Origin and Development 1858-1906* (Agra: Sri Ram Mehra), 1965, p. 158.
18. B.R. Ambedkar, *Pakistan or the Partition of India* (Bombay: Thacker), 1946, p. 242.
19. W.S. Blunt, *India Under Ripon: A Private Diary* (London: T. Fisher Unwin), 1909, pp. 103-04.
20. K.B. Sayed, *Pakistan : The Formative Phase 1857-1948* (London: Oxford University Press), 1968, p. 3.
21. *Ibid.*, pp. 31-32.
22. H.H. Dodwell (ed.), *The Cambridge History of the British Empire,* Vol. 5 (London: Cambridge University Press), 1932, p. 576.
23. John Cunning (ed.), *Political India 1832-1932* (London: Oxford University Press), 1932, p. 88.
24. W.S. Blunt, *India Under Ripon: A Private Diary, op. cit.*, p. 156.
25. Nazir Ahmad, *Ibn ul Waqt* (Lahore: Sheikh Mubarak Ali), 1949, pp. 178-81.
26. Mary, Countess of Minto, *India Minto and Morley* 1905-910, *op. cit.*, p. 383.

27. Jamil-ud-Din Ahmad (ed.), *Speeches and Writings of Mr. Jinnah,* Vol. I (Lahore: Ashraf), 1960, p. 160.
28. R. Palme Dutt, *India Today and Tomorrow* (London: Lawrence and Wishart), 1955, p. 234.
29. *Annual Report of the All India Muslim League for the Year 1932 and 1933,* p. 10.
30. K.B. Sayed, *Pakistan : The Formative Phase 1857-1948, op. cit.*, p. 3.
31. *The Hindustan Times*, Delhi, 30 December 1931.
32. *Annual Report of the All India Muslim League*.
33. Azim Hussain, *Fazl-i-Husain* (Bombay: Longmans), 1946, p. 309.
34. *Ibid.*, p. 312.
35. *The Indian Annual Register* 1938, Vol. I, Calcutta.
36. R. Palme Dutt, *India Today and Tomorrow, op. cit.*, p. 235.
37. *Ibid.*, p. 234.
38. *The Indian Annual Register 1946,* Vol. I, Calcutta.
39. *Annual Report of the All India Muslim League for the Year 1931*, p. 1.
40. Maulan Abul Kalam Azad, *India Wins Freedom* (Calcutta: Longmans), 1959, pp. 160-2
41. *The Indian Annual Register, 1938,* Vol. I, p. 384.
42. Jamil-ud-Din Ahmad (ed.), *Speeches and Writings of Mr. Jinnah,* Vol. I, *op. cit.*, p. 469.
43. Zakir Hussain, Faruqi, *Muslim League Kiyyum*? (Bombay: Maktaha-Sultani), 1947, pp. 230-31.
44. Jamil-ud-Din Ahmad (ed.), *Speeches and Writings of Mr. Jinnah,* Vol. II, *op. cit.*, p. 199.
45. *Ibid.*, p. 245.
46. R. Coupland, *The Indian Problem Part* II (New York: Oxford University Press), 1944, pp. 120-125.
47. *Ibid.*, pp. 91-93.
48. Jamil-ud-Din Ahmad (ed.), *Speeches and Writings of Mr. Jinnah,* Vol. II, *op. cit.*, pp. 132-3.
49. *Dawn*, Delhi, 18 August 1947.
50. K.B. Sayed, *Pakistan : The Formative Phase 1857-1948, op. cit.*, p. 183.
51. Resolutions of the All India Muslim League from March 1941 to April 1942 (Delhi: All India Muslim League, pp. 1-2.
52. K.B. Sayed, *Pakistan : The Formative Phase 1857-1948, op. cit.*, p. 184.

5

TWO-NATION THEORY

Though ideologues claim that Pakistan was born on the day that Muslims first set foot on Indian soil, the first person to systematically set forth the argument for what eventually became Pakistan was the jurist, author, and educator Sir Syed Ahmed Khan (1817-98). He respected, even feared the British, tirelessly arguing that the only way for India's Muslims to resist the encroachment of Christian missionaries and the larger Hindu community was to become educated to a high standard and remain loyal to the Raj. In 1875, Sir Syed laid the basis for what would become Aligarh Muslim University, which in turn produced the scholars and professionals who staffed the Pakistan movement. Although Sir Syed was dedicated to Muslim modernization, Islam's destiny, and the idea of a pan Islamic identity, he stopped short of advocating a separate state for India's Muslims.

Nevertheless, a separate status for India's Muslims was in the works and became an important milestone on the road leading to Pakistan. In the late nineteenth century, the British began to examine more carefully the population they now ruled. Aware of the vast social differences in Indian society, they felt an obligation to protect its vulnerable segments and adopted the principle of separate electorates and quota systems, first for deprived Hindu castes notably the "untouchables" and non-Hindu tribals. Then they acceded to Muslim demands for separate electorates.[1]

The late nineteenth century was the starting period of evolution of two nation theory which caught the imagination of Muslim mind, both at intellectual and at mass level. Much is not known or heard about one Ameer Ali in India. His book *The Spirit of Islam* was published in 1891. He spoke with pride of the past and with hope for the future. He went to the extent of saying that "it can hardly be disputed that real history of India commences with the history of Musalmans".[2] He settled down in London and founded the London branch of the Muslim League in 1908. N.S. Paul, a Caribbean born Indian married to Nadira, a Pakistani Muslim, said that aggressive Islam has a universal tendency to stamp out completely the past civilizational links. Paul's assertion is supported by what Ameer Ali said in 1891.[3]

Maulana Obaidullah, born of Sikh parents in 1872, became an Islamic fundamentalist. He told Gandhi that "India should not be considered as one country, but like Europe it should be divided on linguistic and cultural lines".[4]

The second most important person who fired the imagination of Muslims was Chaudhury Rehmat Ali, a lawyer from Punjab. He spent his entire lifetime for creation of a separate state for Musalmans of India. In fact, it is said that the word Pakistan was coined by him. Muslim ummah was his vision. He was deeply concerned with the shrinking of Islam worldwide and in India. In his booklet *Now or Never* he produced a map of the proposed Pakistan where eight parts of India and two parts of Sri Lanka were to be included as parts of Pakistan.[5]

By introducing a modern Muslim University, the educated Muslims, instead of becoming liberal, ironically became pioneers of the Pakistan movement and propagators of the two nation theory. The Siddon's Club of the Aligarh University in 1887 in a memorandum stated categorically "that religious divisions in India posed a formidable, if not inseparable, obstacle to the evolution of the western style of democracy".[6] The fear was that in a western style of democracy, there would be Hindu domination over Muslims, and that position was not acceptable to Muslims. The logic of melting of religious identities in a democratic system was not liked or cherished. Even if proportionate system of representation was introduced, the same problem of domination theory would be applicable. Sir Ahmed articulated the theory of separateness. He said: "Is it possible ... two nations the Mohamedans and the Hindus could sit on the same throne and remain in power? Most certainly not, it is necessary that one of them should conquer the other and thrust it down. To hope, that both could remain equal, is to derive the impossible and inconceivable."[7] He termed the 1857 revolt as a criminal mutiny and believed that for protection of Muslims the British presence was a guarantee. Jinnah was not wrong when he described the Aligarh Muslim University "as the arsenal of Pakistan". The same tribute was paid by Agha Khan. He said: "The independent sovereign nation of Pakistan was born in the Muslim University of Aligarh".[8]

Coming back to events of significance, it may be recalled that the Muslim League was established in Dhaka in 1906 under the chairmanship of the Nawab of Dhaka. The leaders of Dhaka Muslim League Conference came to the conclusion "that Mohamedans are a distinct community with additional interests of our own which are not shared with other community".[9] On 1 October, 1906 a group of Muslims under Agha Khan met Lord Minto in Simla demanding separate electorate for Muslims. They described themselves as 'the nobles, jagirdars, talukdars, zamindars, lawyers and merchants, subjects of His Majesty the King Emperor in different parts of India.[10] This is the class that led the Pakistan movement subsequently. Minto was highly pleased to accept their basic demands and promised to maintain the partition of Bengal engineered by his predecessor Lord Curzon and the Muslims of Bengal to be rewarded suitably.[11] Thus, the two-nation theory was not Jinnah's creation who entered the mainstream of Muslim politics much later. As aptly said by Akbar S. Ahmed: "Already arguments for Pakistan were being rehearsed", without the ghost of Jinnah hovering around.[12]

The predominantly Hindu Congress did not oppose these seats for so called Mohammedans and in 1916 came to an agreement with the Muslim League on the issue. The Congress and the Muslim League shared other policies as well. Mahatma Gandhi supported the Khilafat movement (the 1919-24 movement that attempted to restore the Ottoman Caliph). This was the first time that a predominately religious issue had been introduced into Indian politics.[13] Interestingly, two of India's leading Muslims, Iqbal and Jinnah, were not involved in the Khilafat movement but were deeply impressed with Turkey's Kamal Ataturk and his regime.

Separate electorates soon became a highly contentious issue, one that remains politically significant even today. India's Muslims, some reasoned, were descendants of peoples who had migrated to the sub-continent several centuries earlier and thus might be considered quite different from indigenous Indians, a separate "nation" and, as such, deserving of protection and a separate electoral status. In the view of others, they were largely converts—their underlying culture, moral values, and social order not unlike those of the "sons of the soil," which meant both groups could share an "Indian" political nationality in a common electoral arrangement.[14]

Swayed by the latter argument, the Congress reversed its position on separate electorates for Muslims although it continued to support them for disadvantaged Hindus and tribals. Troubled by this inconsistency, Indians debated whether there were valid fear for differential treatment of religion, on the one hand, and language, ethnicity, or economic status on the other. To this day, India and Pakistan have been unable to reach a conclusive position on the question of quotas and reservations, as is the case in every state that tries to legislate political equality between economically or socially unequal groups.

Allama Iqbal, the great Urdu poet, is often quoted for bringing an Islamic order in the sub-continent. He is also quoted by Indians for his *Sare jahan se achha Hindostan hamara* which has become almost an unofficial national song. He can be quoted by the rightist, leftists and others for justification of a cause. He was a Kashmiri settled in Punjab. His grandfather, a Sapru Hindu, embraced Islam because of certain compelling reasons. He was the first cousin of Sir Tej Bahadur Sapru. During spare time lqbal used to wear a *dhoti* and relax on a *charpoy*. To mullahs, he was a *kafir* (infidel) for his liberal interpretation of Islam. At one time he wrote *bhajans* and on another occasion he supported the two-nation theory.

The concept of a Muslim 'homeland' was first articulated by Iqbal in his presidential address of the Allahabad session of the Muslim League held on 29 December, 1930. He said: "Punjab, NWFP, Sind and Baluchistan amalgamated into a single state, self-government within the British Empire or without the British Empire, the formation of consolidated north west Indian Muslim state appears to be the final destiny of the Muslims, at least of north west India. Strangely, Iqbal believed that Muslim poverty would be eradicated by enforcement of the laws of Islam. This he said as counter to Nehru's Muslim Mass Contact Movement. Iqbal considered it as a movement "to disrupt Muslim ranks".[15]

In his presidential address, Iqbal gave different reasons for a Muslim homeland in the north west of India. Such a homeland would provide defence of India against foreign aggression. This was a spurious argument as India was always a target of attack by Muslim invaders. The second argument was that free development of Muslims was impossible as Hindus had 'communal dominance' in the whole of India. The real reason for the homeland came from a letter he addressed to Jinnah. He explained why the 1935 Act was not in the interest of the Muslims as "even in the Muslim majority provinces, Muslims are made entirely dependent on non-Muslims."[16] In a way, Iqbal was thinking on the lines of ethnic cleansing.

To distance himself from his Hindu heritage, Iqbal says: "The countries of Islam outside India are practically wholly Muslim in population. The minorities there belong, in the language of Quran, to the 'people of the book'. There are no social barriers between Muslims and the people of the book ... and law of Islam allows intermarriage with the 'people of the book'.[17]

Thus the Partition Idea did not come as a bolt from the blue. Its smoulderings could be seen even towards the close of the nineteenth century. The clash of personalities, the differences in political outlook and the aspiration of the elite of both the communities and the attitude and Interests of the British government played a vital role in widening the gulf between the Hindus and the Muslims.

The dilemma here is that a staunch nationalist and an ambassador of Hindu Muslim unity, Jinnah, became the creator of Pakistan within a short span. An analysis of what caused this U turn in his behaviour would not be out of space here.

Six years younger than Gandhi, Jinnah had also studied law in England, but, unlike Gandhi, his interest outside legal studies had been in politics and not in religion. Jinnah had in his youth come under the influence of Dadabhai Naoroji. He was a friend of

G.K. Gokhale and took to law and politics in Bombay. In his early forties, he was a front-rank politician and took prominent part in the conclusion of the Lucknow Pact in 1916.

Whether in the Imperial Legislative Council of which he was an elected member, or outside, Jinnah's stand on most political problems reflected a spirit of nationalism. He joined the home rule movement and supported the demand for Indian self-government as a condition to whole hearted Indian support to the British government in the war against Germany. In 1919, he condemned the Rowlatt Bill. He criticized the government for its policy in Punjab and towards Turkey, but he did not join Gandhi's movement. The growing influence of Gandhi in Congress in particular and the country in general was not liked by Jinnah. So great was the enthusiasm and respect in the people about Gandhi at the AICC session at Nagpur in 1920 that when Jinnah addressed him as "Mr. Gandhi" he was shouted down by thousands of people, who insisted that he should address him as Mahatma Gandhi.[18]

By this time Jinnah might have realised that there was not much footage left for him in the Congress Party. He nourished this feeling that he had been unfairly edged out of the forefront of the political stage by Gandhi. Louis Fischer records that Jinnah told him, "Nehru worked under me in the home rule society. Gandhi worked under me at the time of the Lucknow Pact". It is doubtless true that in 1916 Jinnah was in the limelight and in 1920 he had almost ceased to be a political force. Several other leaders had a similar experience which is to be attributed to the intensity with which Gandhi's personality and doctrines appealed to millions of Indians who had so far been little affected by politics.

In the twenties Jinnah headed an independent group in the Central Legislative Assembly, where he held the balance between the Congress and the government. His opposition to the solution of the communal problems in the Nehru report went a long way to kill it in 1928. To Gandhi's civil disobedience movement in the early thirties, he took no more kindly than he had done ten years earlier to the non-cooperation movement. At the Round Table Conference, he ploughed a lonely furrow. After the Conference, he almost bade goodbye to Indian politics and settled down in England. But as the time came for the general elections under the new Constitution, he returned to India and led the Muslim League to the polls. The League did not get more than 5 per cent of the Muslim votes. Most of the Hindu organisations were of the opinion that Jinnah had met his Waterloo and he should not be given undue importance. Most of them were of a very definite opinion that when Muslims themselves have rejected Jinnah, he should be ignored. Otherwise, his campaign for separation will get momentum.

From 1937 onwards, a new wave entered Jinnah's speeches and writings, a new desperation which led him from one tactical position to the other until he reached the edge of the precipice. The Congress ministries without the representation of the Muslim League offered him the handiest pegs on which he could deposit all the grievances of Muslims, real or fancied. "The fact is", he declared, "the Congress wants domination of India under the shelter of British bayonets". The Congress was, he alleged, encircling the Muslim League and trying to break up its solidarity. Gandhi was Jinnah's chosen target. "He was the sole dictator and interpreter of the Congress. Gandhi was trying to subjugate and humiliate the Muslims under a Hindu raj, and was trying to annihilate the Muslims, "Jinnah alleged.[19]

In 1939, after the outbreak of the war, the Viceroy invited Gandhi and Jinnah to the palace. Gandhi offered to come to Jinnah house. Jinnah welcomed that appearance of obeisance. But he refused to go in Gandhi's car. They both rode in Jinnah's car. Subsequently, when they conferred, Jinnah insisted that the meeting should take place in his home, Gandhi, who, was completely indifferent to such considerations, gladly compiled.

Vanity, jealousy and dislike undoubtedly play a major role in politics. Some of the great political feuds of the history were personal before they became political. The Hindu Muslim problem to be sure, would have existed, Jinnah or no Jinnah. His intensity and haste blew on the coals and brought forth flames.

To achieve Pakistan Jinnah had to inflame Muslims religious and nationalist sentiments. One of the biggest paradoxes of history is that Jinnah himself was not a religious man but wanted to create a religious state. He used to criticize bitterly the mullahs and other hardcore elements in his community. He used to drink alcohol and ate pork, which are un-Islamic acts, he seldom visited the mosuqe and knew no Arabic and little Urdu. In his forties, he went outside his religion to marry a Parsi girl of 18. His only daughter married a Parsi turned Christian. Hence the irreligious Jinnah wished to build a religious state. Gandhi, wholly religious, wanted a secular state.

1940 Lahore Resolution

Jinnah joined Muslim League in 1913 while retaining his Congress membership. In 1940 in Lahore a resolution was adopted calling for a separate Muslim homeland. The resolution said: "No constitutional plan would be workable in this country or be acceptable to the Muslims, unless it is designed on the following basic principles, namely, that geographically contiguous units are demarcated into regions which should be constituted, with such territorial readjustments as may be necessary, so that the areas in which the Muslims are numerically in a majority, as in the north western and eastern zones of India, are grouped to constitute 'independent states' in which the constituent units shall be autonomous and sovereign."[20]

In his presidential address at the Lahore session he enunciated his "two-nation theory" from the League's platform. He said, "notwithstanding a thousand years of close contact, these nationalities are as divergent today as ever, and they cannot at any time be expected to transform themselves into one nation merely by means of subjecting them to a democratic constitution and holding them forcibly together by the unnatural and artificial methods of British parliamentary statutes."[21]

Several well meaning prominent Muslim leaders criticised the resolution and dissociated themselves from it. Prominent among them were Begum Abdul Aziz, President, Nationalist Muslim Women's Association, Khan Bahadur Allabux, premier of Sindh, Maulana Azad, Sir Habibur Rahman, President, All Bengal Krishak Praja Party, Khan Abdul Qaiyum, who later became Jinnah's lieutenant, and Sir Sikander Hayat Khan, premier of Punjab.

The Hindus and the Sikhs were shocked by the League's resolution. Savarkar, President, All India Hindu Mahasabha, during the course of a speech at Madras on March 26, 1940, said that the Hindu Mahasabha would oppose the division of India into two zones.[22] Jawaharlal Nehru in a speech at Allahabad said, "we will have nothing to do with this mad scheme. The whole problem has taken a new complexion and there is no question of settlement or negotiation."[23]

The nationalist press was equally critical of the Lahore resolution. According to government reports, *Amrit Bazar Patrika* considered the resolution as an absurd scheme. "The child Jinnah has begotten is already dead. Still he hugs it. Only he can, thereby, spite the Congress by proclaiming to the world the disunity between the Hindus and the Muslims."[24]

The adoption of Pakistan resolution on 23 March, 1940 was a well calibrated strategy of Jinnah. His final argument was that even in Muslim majority states, the Muslims had to seek the help of minorities (read Sikhs and Hindus) to form governments, which was not acceptable to Muslim League. Jinnah had an acute sense of timing. In 1934 he told Chaudhary Rehmat Ali: "Don't be in a hurry, let the waters flow and they will find their own level."[25]

Chaudhuri Khaliquzzaman, a Muslim Leaguer from Uttar Pradesh, who seconded the Pakistan resolution said: "If the issue between the Hindus and Muslims is to be decided by means of the sword, the Muslims have no fear."[26]

B.R. Ambedkar lamented that the two-nation theory will not leave room for the growth of that sentimental desire of unity.[27] Rajendra Prasad predicted that "partition is not likely to be attained with the goodwill of those most concerned. This ill will is bound to persist on both sides."[28]

Faizul Haq, who moved the Pakistan Resolution in 1940, a month later called for a united India. He was expelled from the Muslim League in December 1941 as he had formed the ministry in Bengal with the help of a faction of Congress and Mahasabha.

Confusion was created by Abdul Hamid, who chaired Muslim League session in Madras in April 1941. He defined Pakistan as "the establishment of independent and separate Muslim states with a confederating outlook", a vision which would not run "counter to the idea of India's political unity, nor does it mean the vivisection of

India, since the basis of Pakistan had existed all the time in this country."[29] Even at this stage, the clarity on Pakistan Resolution was lacking. On the 1940 Pakistan Resolution, Gandhi expressed his views in *Harijan* on 30 March, 1940. He wrote: "Partition means a patent untruth. My whole soul rebels against the idea that Hinduism and Islam represent two antagonistic cultures and doctrines. To ascent to such a doctrine is for me a denial of God. For I believe with my whole soul the God of Quran is also the God of Gita. I must rebel the idea that the millions who were Hindus the other day changed their nationality on adopting Islam as their religion."[30]

In a very clever way Jinnah was preparing the Muslims for a bloody civil war in the event of non-acceptance of the idea of creation of Pakistan. The next step was very decisive. The Muslim League Working Committee met in Bombay on 15 June, 1940 and decided to issue directions to provincial Muslim Leagues to organize and strengthen the Muslims National Guard Corps "to protect the life and property of Muslims".[31] It was clear that the Muslim League, sooner or later, would launch a civil war, which it ultimately did in August 1946.

The Muslim India concept got wide support from Muslim students all over India. All this has been well documented by Sarfaraz Hussain Mirza in Muslim Students and Pakistan Movement. Some samples of correspondence between the Muslim students and Jinnah/Liaquat are worth reproducing. Maniul Haque Chowdhury of Assam wrote to Jinnah on 10 March, 1943 urging him to visit Assam "to inspire thousands of your sincere and ardent followers with new life". Mujib Ahmad of Sibsagar Muslim Students Federation of Assam wrote to Jinnah on 29 March, 1944 that Pakistan Day was celebrated "with great enthusiasm" and urged Jinnah that Arabic and Persian be introduced in all the girls schools of Assam. A student leader, Mujib Ahmed Moti, in a letter to Jinnah on 3 June, 1944 lamented that the Assamese Muslims were Hindus in thought and action. There were mushrooming of various Muslim Students Forums all over India, including the formation of a student forum called 'Pakistan Students Party'. All these Muslim students fronts were deeply involved in the election campaign in 1946. The Malabar Muslim Students Federation in February 1943 passed a resolution demanding Pakistan as Hindus and Muslims were diametrically opposed to each other. So did the Muslim Students Federation of Bangalore on 27 October, 1943. The atmosphere in Aligarh University was one of Muslim India agitation as witnessed by Roedad Khan, who subsequently became a prominent bureaucrat of Pakistan.

After his release from jail in 1944, the Mahatma unsuccessfully tried to break the deadlock between government and the Congress. Then he sought an accord with Jinnah. The Mahatma did not accept the two nation theory, but he was prepared to realise the psychology which had commended this theory to the Muslim Intelligentsia. The basis on which he prepared to negotiate with Jinnah was the Rajaji 'formula' devised by C. Rajagopalachari.

The Gandhi-Jinnah talks began on September 9, 1944 and concluded on September 27th. The optimism which they aroused at the time only reflected public weariness of the political deadlock, and an almost universal desire for concord between the League and the Congress. On his return from the first interview, Gandhi was asked if he had brought anything from Jinnah: "Only flowers", he replied.[32] The subsequent meetings registered no tangible gains but it recognised the possibility of the Partition of the country.

The fact that Gandhi, who had once described the division of India as a sin, had relented so far as to discuss the machinery for the exercise of the right of self-determination, was a feather in Jinnah's cap. Viewed in the long-term strategy of the campaign for Pakistan, the Gandhi-Jinnah talks were another milestone, marking further progress from the offer of Lord Linlithgow in August 1940, and the Cripps Mission in March 1942.

In the summer of 1945, Lord Wavell put a proposal for the reconstitution of his executive council in consultation with Indian leaders. A conference was convened in Shimla to discuss the proposal. Gandhi was not a delegate to the conference, though he was consulted by the Viceroy and the Congress Working Committee, Lord Wavell had suggested parity of representation in the executive council between the caste Hindus and Muslims, but by the time the conference was over Jinnah was demanding parity between Muslims and all other communities. The conference actually broke down on the insistence of Jinnah that the Muslim League should have an exclusive right to nominate Muslim members of the Viceroy's executive council.

In March 1946, the British government sent a Cabinet Mission to India. Of the three Cabinet members of the mission, Lord Pethick Lawrence and Sir Stafford Cripps were well known to Gandhi. The mission consulted him frequently during their stay both formally and informally.

Prime Minister Attlee was anxious to make the transfer of power not only speedy but smooth. To the British government, the Indian problem was a political problem which was capable of solution by compromise and a spirit of give and take. They were thus committed to no one solution. They were prepared to accept any workable agreement on which the Congress and the League could agree.

Gandhi's view was different. The transfer of power was not a problem of expediency or power politics but one which called for and admitted of a just and moral solution, he wanted the majorities to go far to meet the anxieties of the minorities but he was not prepared to be forced into Partition, which in the long run might do more harm than good to India and the two communities themselves. He was disturbed by the anxiety of the British government not to alienate Jinnah. He advised the Congress not to accept any arrangement in a hurry.

On July 27, 1946, the Muslim League withdrew its acceptance of the Cabinet Mission plan, decided to constitute the constituent assembly and announce a programme of direct action to achieve Pakistan, Jinnah declared that Muslims had bid good bye to constitutional methods. "We have been forced to take to the gun", he said, "and are in a position to use it".[33] The League observed August 16, 1946, 'as direct action day'. On that day Calcutta witnessed communal riots, the scale and intensity of which had never been known in living memory. For four days bands of hoolingans armed with sticks, spears, batchets and even fire arms roamed about in the town, robbing and killing at will. The 'great Calcutta killing', to use the grim epithet coined by *The Statesman*, took a toll of 5,000 lives besides the 15,000 or more who were injured.[34]

Winston Churchill was in secret communication with Mohammad Ali Jinnah and he was tipped off about "Direct Action Day", August 16, 1946, which saw brutal killings by Muslim League activists in Calcutta.

Correspondence recently declassified by the British government indicates a close link between Jinnah and Churchill.[35] The letters relate to the second half of 1946, when Churchill, having lost the 1945 election, was Leader of Opposition.

Gandhi was in Delhi when the news came from East Bengal. He cancelled all his programmes and decided to leave for East Bengal. Friends tried to dissuade him. His health was poor. "I do not know", he said, "what I shall be able to do there. All that I know is that I won't be at peace unless I go". Accordingly, he went there and did whatever he could.[36]

In the meantime, Lord Mountbatten succeeded Lord Wavell as Viceroy. One of the first acts of the Viceroy was to invite Gandhi for a discussion. The Mahatma interrupted his peace mission in Bihar and travelled to New Delhi. He advised Mountbatten to dissolve the Congress League coalition government and to ask Jinnah to form a cabinet. Evidently, Gandhi's object was to disarm Jinnah's suspicion of the Congress and Hindus with one supreme gesture. To the British government, however, the suggestion looked far fetched. The Congress leaders had lately seen enough of their Muslim League colleagues in the interim government. When Jinnah met Mountbatten, he reiterated his demand for the division of India.

After a few months of stormy courtship with the League in the interim government, the Congress was forced to reorient its attitude towards Partition. In the spring of 1947, the choice seemed to them to be between anarchy and Partition. They resigned themselves to the latter in order to salvage three-fourth of India from the chaos which threatened the whole.

Though vaguely conceived, the idea of Pakistan did tie together the three major Muslim communities of British India: those of East Bengal, Punjab, and the United Provinces. The Pakistan movement was not strong in the Northwest Frontier Province or Sindh, or in India's south. For seven years, from the passage of the Lahore Resolution demanding a separate Pakistan in 1940 to independence in 1947, the differences between these groups were contained by Jinnah's leadership. He negotiated both with the British and with the Indian nationalists, winning enough victories at the polls to make the claim for Pakistan credible.

Jinnah was fortunate in that the other two players in the drama were, at their core, liberal. The Raj was a far cry from the brutal French regime in Algeria, the Dutch in Indonesia, or the Portuguese in Africa. The Indian National Congress, too, was a liberal organization; like the Muslim League, it was led by a lawyer, and its firebrands were marginalized. While the League's fight for Pakistan has been mythologized as a titanic battle against two implacable foes, the Raj and the Congress, it was in fact not much of a struggle. This has contributed a great deal to Pakistan's later inclination towards constitutional structures and the rule of law even when it has been unable to sustain them.

As the economist scholar Shahid Javed Burki notes, "The new state was meant to achieve different things for different people: emancipation from the Hindu landlords of the peasantry of Bengal and Assam; the creation of new economic and political opportunities for the frustrated urban Muslim classes of Delhi, Bombay, and the United and Central provinces; and the establishment of an Islamic state" for the religiously minded in Sindh, Punjab, and the Northwest Frontier Province.[37] Pakistan as an idea was successful enough to command support from many, but not all, of India's Muslims; as a blueprint for a state, it was to lounder on the rocks of these different interests.

Ironically, a decision by the Indian National Congress helped turn the idea of Pakistan, a long shot or a negotiating tactic at best, into reality. Whereas the Congress had supported Britain in World War I, in 1942 its members, led by Gandhi, decided to launch the "Quit India" movement and sat out the war in prison, demanding a promise of independence in exchange for their support. Some prominent members even sympathized with the Axis powers. As a result, the British relied on the Muslim League to help them recruit soldiers to the Indian army. Punjabi Muslims were the single largest recruitment class in the army that gathered Indian Muslims to its own cause.

The Congress's non-participation in the war made the British wary. Those in military and strategic circles in particular had to look after post-war British imperial interests and vastly distrusted Gandhi and the Congress Party. Though India was no longer the jewel in the imperial crown, Britain still had colonies to India's east and precious oil reserves to its west. There was also some concern that India, led by the "leftist" Nehru, might fall under Soviet influence.

The idea of Pakistan as an independent, pro-Western state remaining under Western (that is, British) tutelage was thus quite attractive. For many British strategists, the most secure foothold would be in an independent Pakistan, with its loyal army and Western leaning Muslim League leadership.[38] Whereas Pakistanis tend to emphasize the injustices and discrimination that made separation necessary, Indian historians tend to regard Pakistan as partly the product of this British imperial strategy, not the result of a legitimate demand. The historical record is complex and rich enough to support both interpretations, and as with so many other events that conceptually divide the two states, debate continues to surround the partition of British India.

When two cultures collide, does one flee from the other, accommodate it, ignore it, absorb it, yield to it, or try to destroy it?[39] Most Muslim rulers on the sub-continent eventually accommodated their Hindu subjects, but the coming of the British opened up the question once again, particularly for Muslims. Since Hindus took to British education more readily than Muslims, many Muslim elites felt overwhelmed by a devastating coalition of British power and renascent Hinduism, which had been energized by the tools of learning and power acquired from the British. Not only had the Hindus transformed themselves but their numbers were so great that Muslims could not even hope to maintain normal relations with them, which could only be realized if Muslims had equal status or access to skills, positions, and assets that would protect their special position in India. Perhaps, there was also some fear of Hindu revenge for crimes chronicled by Alberuni and others.

Though Iqbal may have considered Pakistan part of a larger Islamic rebirth, the spirit behind it also resembled the nation state movement of the nineteenth century, as reflected in Zionism or the

Armenian national movement. More recent comparisons would include the Chechnyan, Bosnian, and Palestinian movements, which also seek homelands for oppressed minorities, and which have been strongly supported by Pakistan. The Indian National Congress, which made the comparison with Israel, noted that both Zionism and the Pakistan movement identified their members by religion and professed tolerance for religious minorities within the borders of the new state. Where they differ is that Israel opens its doors to all coreligionists while Pakistan restricts entry of Muslims from India and even Bangladesh. Even Jinnah did not foresee Pakistan as a homeland for all of India's Muslims.

By making religion the basis for a separate nation state, argued Pakistani nationalists, the new Muslim homeland would also be a progressive state because Islam, unlike Hinduism, is a modern religion with a proud position in history as the faith that brought to perfection the religions of the modern, advanced, scientific West, Judaism and Christianity. Islam is part of this tradition, whereas Hinduism belongs to another world, that of the complete non-believer. In the extreme view, Hindus lack even the revelations of the other "people of the book"; their accomplishments were historically interesting but are not to be regarded as modern or progressive.

This distinction between the world of Islam (in Arabic, world of submission or peace) and the remainder of mankind is central to Islamic political thought. Pakistani ideologues believe that the acceptance of Islam and proper guidance enable man to create a society of peace and justice on this earth. By contrast, they contend, Hindus believe that Islam offers no hope of perfection, for the world is in an era of decay and destruction, i.e., Kaliyug. In this scheme of things, individual redemption through death and rebirth is a difficult and slow process. Hindus profess no real faith, only a cynical opportunism and a crude and misguided devotion to a thousand gods. As some Muslims argued at the time of separation, if they could not rule over Hindus, then they had to be shielded from Hindu influence, not by becoming a separate and equal society, but a separate and superior one.

For the more ardent supporters of Pakistan, the structure of the Hindu caste system was further empirical evidence of the incompatibility between Islam and Indian culture and of the need for a separate state. Like many non-Hindus, they associated caste with *varna*, Hinduism's theoretical four-fold social hierarchy. At the same time, some Pakistanis prided themselves on Rajput or other high caste origins, although a great number were converts to Islam from lower Hindu castes. Thus, they harboured a special resentment toward "Hindu Brahmin" dominance and arrogance flowing from being at the top of the system. Equally important in elite Pakistani circles was the view that regional discord stems from the "Hindu mind," which is often characterized as scheming and devious, and compelled to expand.[40]

Thus, the idea of Pakistan rests on the elite Indian Muslim sense of being culturally and historically distinct. This view descends in part from the original Muslim invaders of the sub-continent, and in part from the willingness of some to abandon corrupt Hinduism for a peaceful and just Islam.

Although Islam is an egalitarian religion, the leadership of the Pakistan movement had difficulty accepting the democratic norm of one man, one vote. Jinnah and others tirelessly argued that without some restraint on majority power, Muslims would always be outvoted. Once the British left, who would check the majority Hindu community? Jinnah strongly opposed independence if it meant representative government based on numbers: "three to one," three Hindus for every Indian Muslim. Who, he asked, would interpret and enforce the terms of the transfer of power from Britain to India? "We come back to the same answer: the Hindu majority would do it, and will it be with the help of the British bayonet or Mr. Gandhi's *Ahimsa* [strategy of non-violence]? Can we trust them any more?[41] Unyieldingly, Jinnah's answer was no, no, and again no. Sarcastically, he threw back Gandhi's claim that the two men were brothers, that Hindus, Muslims, Parsis, Harijans are all alike: "The only difference is this, that brother Gandhi has three votes and I have only one vote."[42]

As far as Jinnah was concerned, "a thousand years of close contact, nationalities which are as divergent today as ever cannot at any time be expected to transform themselves into one nation merely by means of subjecting them to a democratic constitution."

And, Jinnah added, Muslims were not even minorities as the term is "commonly known and understood," since they were a majority in four of eleven British Indian provinces.

The two nation theory movement bequeathed to the state of Pakistan a number of identities.[43] First, Pakistan was clearly "Indian," in that the strongest supporters of the idea of Pakistan identified themselves as culturally Indian, although in opposition to Hindu Indians. This Indian dimension of Pakistan's identity has been systematically overlooked by contemporary Pakistani politicians and scholars. Even Pakistan's Buddhist heritage is ignored, even though twelve hundred years before the arrival of Mohd. bin Qasim in Sindh, people in great numbers from the soil what now form Bangla Desh and Pakistan beyond had embraced Buddhism and present-day Pakistan has many impressive Buddhist pilgrimage sites.

Second, the idea of Pakistan implied that Pakistan would be a modern extension of the great Islamic empires of South Asia, whose physical remnants still dominate the subcontinental landscape.

Third, Pakistan was also a legatee of British India, sharing in the 200-year-old tradition of the Raj. This itself was a complex identity, as British India had incorporated Turkish, Persian, and Hindu practices into its own structure.

Fourth, because of its cultural links with Central Asia, strategies such as Jinnah viewed Pakistan was to be a boundary between the teeming masses of India and the vastness of Central Asia. Such a Pakistan, with its strong military tradition, was to serve as the guardian of South Asia. In subsequent years, Pakistani strategists and their American and British counterparts came to see Pakistan as a balance to both the then Soviet Union and the pro-Soviet government of India (eventually, China came to hold the same view).

Fifth, since Pakistan was also to be part of the Islamic world, it would share in one way or another the ummah's destiny. As a result, it had a special interest in the persecution of Muslim minorities in the rest of the world. Pakistan was, in brief, blessed with many assets, several great traditions, and a number of potential identities. It was Jinnah who wove these attributes together, arguing that without a separate Muslim homeland, South Asia would be mired in conflict and vulnerable to outside pressure. For him, the past pointed to the future.

REFERENCES

1. Stephen Philip Cohen, *The Idea of Pakistan* (New Delhi: Oxford University Press), 2005, p. 25.
2. S. K. Datta and Rajeev Sharma, *Pakistan From Jinnah to Jehad* (New Delhi: UBSPD), 2002, p. 7.
3. *Ibid.*
4. Aziz Beg, *Jinnah and His Times* (Karachi: Babur and Amer Publications), 1986, p. 104.
5. Chaudhary Rahmat Ali, *Pakistan: The Farther Land of Pak Nation* (London: The Pak National Liberal Movement), 1947, p. 235.
6. S.K. Datta, and Rajeev Sharma, *Pakistan from Jinnah to Jehad*, *op. cit.*, p. 8.
7. Richard Symonds, *Making of Pakistan* (London: Faber and Faber), 1950, p. 31.
8. Aziz Beg, *Jinnah and His Times*, *op. cit.*, p. 104.
9. K.B. Sayeed, *Pakistan: The Formative Phase 1857-1948* (London: Oxford University Press), 1968, p. 28.
10. *Ibid.*
11. Mary Countess of Minto, *India Minto and Morely 1905-1910* (London: Macmillan), 1934, p. 47.
12. Akbar, Ahmad, *Jinnah Pakistan and Islamic Identity* (London: Routledge), 1997, p. 110.
13. Hamza Alavi, "Parting of the Ways", in Zubeida Mustafa (ed.), *The South Asian Century: 1900-1999* (London: Oxford University Press), 2000, p. 16.
14. Peter Hardy, "Modern European and Muslim explanations of Conversion to Islamic in South Asia" in Nehemia Lentizion (ed.), *Conversion to Islam* (New York: Holmes and Meir), 1979, p. 69.
15. G.H. Zulfikar, *Pakistan: As Visualised by Iqbal and Jinnah* (Lahore: Bajm-e-Iqbal), 1989, p. 28.
16. *Ibid.*, p. 34.
17. *Ibid.*, p. 23.
18. Subhash Chandra Bose, *The Indian Struggle Part II* (Calcutta: Published for Netaji Publishing Society), 1945, p. 162.
19. Jai Narain Sharma, "Irreligious Jinnah Wanted a Religious Pak", *The Tribune*, Chandigarh, 6 July 1997.
20. S.S. Pirzada (ed.), *Foundations of Pakistan*, All India Muslim League Documents 1906-1947 (Karachi: National Publishing House), 1969, p. 341.
21. *Ibid.*
22. O.P. Ralhan (ed.), *Hindu Mahasabha*, Vol. II (New Delhi: Anmol), 1997.
23. Jai Narain Sharma, "Irreligious Jinnah Wanted a Religious Pak", *op. cit.*
24. *Amrit Bazar Patrika*, 24 March 1940.
25. Sikander Hayat, *Pakistan Resolution Revisited* (Islamabad: National Institute of Historical and Cultural Research), 1999, p. 87.
26. Latif Ahmad, Sherwani, *Pakistan Resolution to Pakistan* (Delhi: Daya Publishing House), 1985, p. 23.

27. B.R. Ambedkar, *Pakistan or the Partition of India* (Bombay: Thacker & Co.), 1946, pp. 85-87.
28. *The Tribune*, Lahore, 29 August 1940.
29. Anita Inder Singh, *The Origin of the Partition of India 1936-47* (Bombay: Oxford University Press), 1987, p. 75.
30. *Ibid.*, p. 59.
31. Aziz Beg, *Jinnah and His Times, op. cit.*, p. 560.
32. Jai Narain Sharma, "Irreligious Jinnah Wanted A Religious Pak", *op. cit.*
33. *Ibid.*
34. *Ibid.*
35. *The Indian Express,* Chandigarh, 9 August 2005.
36. Jai Narain Sharma, "Irreligious Jinnah Wanted a Religious Pak", *op. cit.*
37. Shahid Javed Burki, *Pakistan, The Continuing Struggle for Nationhood* (Boulder Colo. West View Press), 1991, pp. 22-23.
38. Nicholas Mansergh, E.W.R. Lumby and Penderel Moon, *The Transfer of Power 1942-47* (London; Her Majesty Stationery Office), 1970-83.
39. Ainslie T. Embree, *Imaging India: Essays on Indian History* (London: Oxford University Press), 1989, Ch. 3.
40. Javed Hassan, *India: A Study in Profile* (Rawalpindi: Army Book Service), 1990.
41. S.S. Pirzada (ed.), *Foundations of Pakistan*, All India Muslim League Documents 1906-1947, *op. cit.*
42. Stephen Philip Cohen, *The Idea of Pakistan, op. cit.*, pp. 36-37.
43. *Ibid.*

6

WAS JINNAH SECULAR?

Was Jinnah secular? This question is being hotly debated in India today. While answering this question in the present chapter, I have followed the dictum of famous British Editor C.P. Scott, who wrote, "Facts are sacred; comment is free." I have not made any of my own comments but have tried to put the facts before the readers who can draw their own conclusions.

Jinnah who ate pork, drank scotch, seldom entered a mosque, was ignorant of Islamic teachings, did not observe Islamic rituals, could not speak Urdu, wore high class Western suits and had come from a Hindu family, was Christened Quaid-e-Azam by the Muslim Maulvis. After he came to be recognized the leader of the Pakistan movement, frantic efforts were made to give Jinnah a new image. The Muslim feudal lords and the capitalists showered money for this purpose and the intellectuals applied their brain to paint Jinnah's new picture. The *Star of India* and *Dawn* were foremost in this effort. Jinnah was characterized as the greatest figure in Islamic history, next to the Holy Prophet and the uncrowned king of the Muslims of India.

To identify himself with this new role, Jinnah had already started preparations. He discarded his Western clothes, learnt Urdu, attended Muslim League meetings in *Achkan* and tight trousers. When he visited Punjab and the North Western Frontier, he sported Punjabi *salwar* to give the impression that he was one of them. In conservative areas, he would make sure that his sister Fatima who did not wear the veil, was not seated with him. Not known to have a passion for Namaz, the Id Day saw him faithfully bending with the low and the poor and the rich in the Azad Maidan, Bombay.[1] He accompanied the huge procession numbering 20,000 at Gaya in Bihar in which swords and other weapons were carried and received a sword and a copy of the Koran from Pesh Imam of Jama Masjid. He bade goodbye to constitutional means and announced 'direct action day' which was followed by a Hindu Muslim riot in Calcutta on an unprecedented scale leading to arson, rape, looting and killings of both Hindus and Muslims.[2] He gave up the idea of Indian unity and preached newly adopted ideology. He said:

"Religion is considered not merely religion, in the strict sense as understood in the West by a Hindu or a Muslim, but a complete social order which affects all the activities of life. In Islam, religion is the motive spring of all actions in life. A Muslim of one country has far more sympathies with a Muslim living in another country than with a non-Muslim living in the same country.... Even now an Indian Muslim feels far more stirred by the distress of his Muslim brothers beyond India than by a similar calamity affecting non-Muslims in India."[3]

Emphasising the importance of religion, Jinnah argued: "Religion alone is a cohesive force for the idea of a nationality. In countries where the allegiance of people is divided on the basis of religion, the idea of a single nationality has never finally succeeded. In Germany, the Christians and Jews have lived together for centuries and yet they failed to weld together into a single nation."[4]

In expanding this fundamental assumption of nationhood, he explained:

"You must remember that Islam is not merely a religious doctrine but a realistic and practical code of conduct. I am thinking in terms of life, of everything important in life. I am thinking in terms of our history, our heroes, our art, our architecture, our music, our laws, our jurisprudence.... In all these things our outlook is not only fundamentally different but often radically antagonistic to the Hindus. We are different beings. There is nothing in life which links us together. Our names, our clothes, our foods, these are all different; our economic life, our educational ideas, our treatment of women, our attitude to animals, we challenge each other at every time of the compass. Take one example, the internal question of the cow.

We eat the cow, the Hindus worship it. A lot of Englishmen imagine that this worship is merely a picturesque convention, an historical survival. It is nothing of the sort. Only a few days ago, in this very city, the cow question became a matter for the police. The Hindus were thrown into the greatest agitation because cows were being killed in public. But the cow question is only one of a thousand."[5]

With this new rhetoric and single minded propaganda, Jinnah established himself as a potent force in the then political situation of the country. The membership of the Muslim League increased tremendously and it claimed to have two million members. It also got electoral victories. In the sixty-one provincial bye elections filled by separate electorates between 1937 and 1943, the Muslim League won forty-seven.[6] This victory made him the undisputed leader of the Muslim League which in turn became his lengthened shadow.

After acquiring this strength, Jinnah claimed to be the sole spokesman of the Muslims in India. There were Muslims in the Congress, the Communist Party, the Congress Socialist Party, the Radical Democratic League of M.N. Roy and in the Forward Bloc, but Jinnah did not regard them representative of the Muslim community. For him, they were mere show boys and were misguided. He demanded that the Muslim League be recognized as the sole authoritative organization. The British readily recognised his claim and Congress too conceded. It stated:

"The Congress does not challenge, and accept the Muslim League now as the authoritative representative of the overwhelming majority of the Muslims of India. As such, and in accordance with democratic principles, they alone have today the unquestionable right to represent the Muslims of India."[7]

His attitude towards Gandhi hardened and acquired a new dimension. He gave up his earlier stance of pleading with Gandhi and seeking meetings with him. The Viceroy had called a conference at Simla of party leaders on August 9, 1944 to which Gandhi and Jinnah were invited. At Simla someone suggested to Jinnah that it might be desirable if he and Gandhi could meet before meeting the Viceroy. Jinnah agreed but added, "I am willing to see him if he wishes, but I am not willing that you should say that I wish to see him."[8] Gandhi, when approached, replied: "If I were to say that I wish to see Jinnah, it would be a lie. But if Jinnah wishes to meet me, I will walk barefoot from here to Cecil Hotel."[9]

Pakistan was a trump card in his hands to dictate his terms to the Congress otherwise he had no special love for his community. He refused to lend any support to any campaign launched by Muslims belonging to other political parties, for the upliftment of the poor Muslim masses. One such campaign was the literacy campaign launched by the Bombay Municipal Corporation. It had established night schools all over the city. Those in the Muslim localities were placed under the supervision of Mrs. Kulsum Sayani, a Congress member and a well known social worker. Kulsum Sayani wished to secure the moral support of the Muslim League for an activity beneficial to Muslims and about which there could be no controversy. M.R.A. Baig writes:

"One night, therefore, we took Mr. Jinnah for a tour of the night schools, we took him to places he never knew existed, and he delightfully climbed up dirty, narrow stairs to dark, dingy rooms. But we failed in our mission. At the end he thanked us politely, told Kulsum Sayani that she was doing good work, but refused to direct the Muslim League to support the adult literacy campaign."[10] The reasons were obvious. The corporation was in Congress control, and it was not for him and the Muslim League to help them to get any credit or popularity among the Muslim public. That the Muslim public benefited or not did not matter.[11] He was interested in the Muslim League and not the Muslims.

By nature Jinnah could never be subservient to anyone. He refused to do things he did not want to do merely to please the Muslim people. Aziz Beg writes about such an incident: "Wavell, the British Viceroy, called a conference of Indian leaders to meet him in Simla, the summer capital of the Government. Having alighted from the narrow gauge train, he sat in a rickshaw to go to his hotel. As he approached the hub of the city, thousands of people had gathered to greet him. A Muslim League worker suddenly stepped forward and implored Jinnah to remove his white sola hat as it was Western headgear. Jinnah snubbed him and said, 'Now that almost everybody has seen me, you want them also to see me put off the hat, just to please them.' "[12]

"I was always amazed," reminisces M.R.A. Baig, "by the way he sometimes refused to play up even to his followers. I remember once sitting with him when a servant announced that some Muslims wished to see him. Looking annoyed he said, "send them in." They came in, simple fellows and awestruck before the great man, huddled in a group, snuffing their feet. "Well," he said, in English, "what do you want?" "Sahib" one replied in Urdu, "We have come to see you." "Well, you have seen me," he replied in English, and turned his chair and resumed our discussion.[13]

Baig had intimate relations with Jinnah. He left the Muslim League after Pakistan Resolution. He writes about one such incident: "A crowd had gathered at the Railway Station to welcome his arrival. As happens sometimes, they got a little unruly. Furious, he pulled down the shutters and refused to come out till they had been dispersed."[14]

Even after assuming the role of Quaid-e-Azam, he maintained distance and remained aloof not only from the Muslim masses but also the Muslim leaders. Begum Liaqat Ali Khan recalls an incident when, during his visit to Baluchistan, he avoided shaking hands with people. She reminisces: "He attended a garden party where he had to meet hundreds of people. Among them was an old chieftain, a Muslim Sirdar who advanced towards Jinnah and held out his hands. Jinnah, in a sudden mood of aloofness said, if I shake hands with you, I would have to shake hands with all the people here, and for that there is no time."[15]

Hector Bolitho, his biographer, also writes about an incident that shows that Jinnah did not care about the Muslim Leaguer's views and many a time snubbed them. Once when some members of the Muslim League told him that he should travel in third class on the railway, as Gandhi did, he was furious. He said, "Do not dictate to me what I should do or should not do. It is not your money I am spending, and I shall live and act as I choose."[16]

He, in his own words, had only Hindu friends and enjoyed his aristocratic living. He was misfit among the Muslim social gatherings. Khurshid narrates such an incident in his book *Memories of Jinnah*: "In the end of January 1944 Jinnah was in Kashmir, Mir Waiz Maulvi Mohd. Yusuf had given a party for the members of the Muslim

Conference Council. The meal was served in the traditional Kashmiri way. A huge metal rakaba or dish heaped with plain boiled rice, enough to feed six, was placed before Mr. Jinnah. Everyone was seated on the floor and it had not occurred to the host to provide cutlery as rice is always eaten with one's fingers in the traditional way. Mr. Jinnah felt rather embarrassed but then the situation was saved when someone produced a spoon with which the Quaid-e-Azam helped himself to some rice, washing it down with a glass of soda water."[17]

He even did not have a high opinion of Muslims. He told Qazi Isa when the latter went to call on Jinnah in New Delhi in July 1945. "It is always among the Muslims that you find traitors."[18]

M.C. Chagla once asked Jinnah, "You are fighting for Pakistan mainly in the interest of the Muslim majority states. But what happens to the Muslims in states particularly like Uttar Pradesh, where they are in a small minority." He looked at me for a while and said: "They will look after themselves. I am not interested in their fate."[19]

Major General Shahid Hamid also shared the above view. He had invited Jinnah to his house on August 3, 1947. An officer asked Jinnah about the prospect of promotion in Pakistan. Jinnah replied angrily, "You Mussalmans, either you are up in the sky or down in the dumps. You cannot adopt a steady course."[20]

Thus, for Jinnah, Pakistan was a bargaining counter to settle his personal accounts with the Congress and to humble its leaders who had questioned even his representative character and had tried to finish him politically. Penderel Moon, who was in the confidence of the Muslim leaders of Punjab, writes in his book *Divide and Quit* that privately Jinnah told one or two people in Lahore that this Pakistan resolution was a "tactical move; and the fact that six years later he was ready to accept something less than absolute partition suggests that in 1940 he was not really irrevocably committed to it."[21] Kanji Dwarkadas had a ninety minutes talk with Jinnah on August 28, 1942. He shared the above view. He says that "Jinnah was not thinking in terms of Pakistan. Nor did he think of becoming the Head of a new State of Pakistan. In fact Jinnah never imagined that Pakistan would ever come into being."[22]

The Secret Official Records of the British Government also state the same view. The Director of Intelligence at Government Headquarter prepared a very detailed paper on this subject and opined that "Jinnah has never really intended to have a separate Pakistan. He has used it as a propaganda weapon to win concessions from the Congress."[23]

Correspondence recently declassified by the British government indicates a close link between Jinnah and Churchill.[24] The letters relate to the second half of 1946, when Churchill, having lost the 1945 election, was Leader of Opposition. Winston Churchill was in secret communication with Mohammad Ali Jinnah and he was tipped off about "Direct Action Day", August 16, 1946, which saw brutal killings by Muslim League activists in Calcutta.

In the letters, Jinnah seems to warm Churchill about imminent violence. As riots broke out all over India and the Labour government —led by Churchill's rival Clement Atlee—sought to hurriedly transfer power, Churchill played counsellor to Jinnah, but privately. He advised Jinnah that they should not meet in public. Instead, correspondence was to be addressed to "Miss E.A. Gilliatt, 6 Westminster Gardens, London." Gillaitt was Churchill's private secretary.

The letters reveal Jinnah saw Churchill as an ally against "Caste Hindus". The Conservative wartime leader—hostile to the "liquidation of the British Empire"—was told by the Muslim League leader on July 6, 1946, that the Cripps Mission had "Shaken the confidence of Muslim Indians and shattered their hopes for an honourable and peaceful settlement".

Jinnah wrote, "If power politics are going to be the deciding factor in total disregard for fair play and justice, we shall have no other course open to us except to forge our sanctions to meet the situation which, in that case, is bound to arise. Its consequence, I need not say, will be most disastrous and a peaceful settlement will then become impossible." Less than six weeks later came the bloodbath of Direct Action.

Replying to Jinnah on August 5, Churchill "espoused the right of Moslems and the Depressed Classes to their fair share of life and power. I feel that it is most important that the British Army should not be used to dominate the Moslems, even though the caste Hindus might claim numerical majority in a constituent assembly".

On August 22, Jinnah wrote again to Churchill's domestic opponents, the Labour Party, which Jinnah felt was Congress-friendly, "You admit the tendencies in England to support the Congress are very strong in the Government Party," Jinnah wrote, "We have had a bitter taste of it".

The Muslim League was progressively betrayed by the Cabinet Delegation and the Viceroy and was being gradually steam-rolled. When the Secretary of State for India and his colleagues and the Viceroy finally disclosed their hands, undoubtedly, there could be only one result and that is a general revolt against the British. For who else is responsible to force down and thrust upon 100 million Muslims of India terms which the Congress alone will be pleased to accept.

The argument on the British-Muslim relationship was an old one. On August 3, Churchill had written to Jinnah, "I was surprised to read all the insulting things that were said about Britain at the Moslem congress in Bombay, and how the Moslems of India were described as undergoing British slavery. All this is quite untrue and ungrateful."

But on December 12, a wary Churchill turned down a lunch invitation at the Claridges's, advising that the two should not be "associated publicly".

Lord Mountbatten also confirms the above view. While recording the talk, Mountbatten remarked: "He gives me the impression of a man who has not thought out one single piece of the mechanics of his own scheme, and he really will get the shock of his life when he comes down to earth."[25]

Acceptance of partition by the Congress was a rude shock of his life. He became speechless and when asked by Mountbatten, he just nodded his head in approval. Thus he became the victim of his own politics. It is also said that after agreeing to divide, Jinnah met Mountbatten again and said that he did not want Pakistan but would be content with an honourable settlement with the Congress and the British Government in a United India. Mountbatten snubbed Jinnah and said it was too late to think of an alternative.[26]

Jinnah did not forgive Mountbatten for this insult. Perhaps this episode led him to oppose common Governor Generalship of Mountbatten and he decided to become the Governor-General of Pakistan himself. Mountbatten had assured the British Government that Jinnah would opt for a common Governor-General and he honestly believed he would; Jinnah's decision, therefore seemed a personal insult to him. Not only this, Jinnah did not go to the Airport to welcome Mountbatten when the latter along with his wife Lady Edwina came to Karachi to proclaim the end of the British Empire by giving oath of office to Jinnah, the new Governor-General of Pakistan.[27] Jinnah could not make a retreat and Pakistan came into existence. Jinnah was "too proud to publicly admit his blunder."[28]

M.N. Roy, Jinnah's contemporary and leader of the Democratic League opines: "Mohammad Ali Jinnah was the most maligned and misunderstood man. That experience made him bitter and it was very largely out of spitefulness that he pursued an object, the attainment of which placed him in the most difficult position. Jinnah was not an idealist in the sense of being visionary; he was a practical man possessed of great shrewdness as well as of more than average intelligence. Such a man could not be blind to the difficulty which was to follow his highly problematical success. During the latter part of his career, politics was a gamble for him; having played a game of poker with high stakes, he could not pull out. He had to go to the bitter end, so to say. Bitter, because he must have been frightened by the spectre of success, when it came within the reach of possibility. But then it was too late to retreat. It was a case of a man getting inextricably entangled in power politics without having begun with the lust for political power. Few would agree yet, that is a fact which will win the recognition of impartial and dispassionate historians."[29]

M.N. Roy argues further: "Indeed, the homeland for the Indian Muslims was a utopia, any territorial division was bound to leave many millions of them out in a very delicate position of being regarded as aliens, suspected of disloyalty to the land they must live in. An intelligent man like Jinnah must have foreseen the tragic consequence of what he demanded. Therefore, I do not believe that he really wanted partition of the country. Like a gambler overconfident of his wits, he staked high, believing that the other party would compromise on his terms. That would have been for the best of all concerned. But the latter having taken up the attitude of all or nothing, Jinnah was driven to the bitter end of gaining a victory he himself dreaded and which he did not survive."[30]

The achievement of Pakistan, however, did not make him the hero of all the Muslim communal and separatist forces. He was bitterly criticised and called a traitor by not less a person than Rahmat Ali himself. Jinnah had borrowed his ideal, his arguments and his nomenclature without even naming him. Rahmat Ali issued a pamphlet on June 9, 1947 regarding Pakistan and the main target of attack was Jinnah.

The incredible has happened. In its life and death struggle, the blackest treachery has been committed against the Millat. To his crying shame, to his consuming agony of the Millat, and to the contemptuous joy of the British Bania Alliance, Mr. Jinnah followed by the All India Muslim League, has accepted the British Plan of 3rd of June 1947. ... In accepting the British Plan Mr. Jinnah has acted the Judas and betrayed, bartered and dismembered the Millat.[31]

Rahmat further wrote: "Jinnah is befooling the Muslims into hailing their miserable fate as good fortune, and their betrayal by him as a blessing.... Little does he realize that, by doing this, he is adding the smear of shame to the sorrow of disaster suffered by Islam; that he is sprinkling salt on the gaping wounds inflicted by him on the body of Millat... his crime is too black to be whitewashed ... its consequences are too calamitous to be forgotten by the Millat ... his attempts are too crude to deceive history."[32]

Before leaving India Jinnah made a last appeal to both Hindus and Muslims to "bury the past" and wished India success and prosperity.[33] Thus the 'sole spokesman' of the Muslims safely migrated to Pakistan on August 7, 1947 leaving behind the five crores of Muslims to wallow in the mire of bloodshed.

Now that he had got Pakistan, he decided to make it a model country, a truly democratic and modern state based on Hindu-Muslim unity and a fair share to all the minorities. He did not want to build the new state on Islamic principles. In fact, he had already made it clear to the Mullahs. In 1944, the Ahrars offered to support Jinnah provided he gave assurance that the State of Pakistan would be based on Islamic principles. Jinnah turned down their offer. Even before leaving India for Pakistan Jinnah repeated this. According to Iskandar Mirza: "Before we all left Delhi, I said to the Quaid-e-Azam one day, 'Sir we are all agreed to go to Pakistan; but what kind of polity are you going to have? Are you going to have an Islamic State?' 'Nonsense' he replied, I am going to have a modern state."[34]

He told Sri Prakasa, the first Indian High Commissioner to Pakistan that he intended to make Pakistan a secular state. He had no longer any grudge against anyone. In fact, he was anxious to revert to his old and familiar role of Ambassador of Hindu Muslim unity. He proposed that he should continue as the champion of minorities in Pakistan as he had been, for several years now, the champion of the minorities in India.[35]

He tried to dispel all doubts and suspicions about the polity and principles of the new state. In the Press Conference which was held on July 13, 1947 in the backyard of his house at 10 Aurangzeb Road, every newspaper was represented. "Minorities to whichever community they may belong, will be safeguarded. Their religion or their faith or belief will be protected in every way possible. Their life and property will be secure. There will be no interference of any kind with their freedom of worship. They will have their protection with regard to their religion, their faith, their life, their property, their culture. They will be in all respects the citizens of Pakistan without any distinction of caste or colour, religion or creed." He further said, "as long as I have any power, they need have no apprehension of any kind."[36]

M.S.M. Sharma questioned Jinnah, "Had you not stated in the past, Mr. Jinnah, that there should be an exchange of population between India and Pakistan. Of course now, the division of the country would be followed by processions of Muslims from this country and Hindus from the other side."[37]

"You are mistaken," declared Jinnah. The old demand for the exchange of population was outdated. It had no force now. They had agreed to divide as brothers. There was no trail of bitterness. There could be no question of any exchange of population. Hindus of Pakistan will have to live in Pakistan and the Muslims of India will have to live in India, he averred."[38]

The next question was what kind of treatment awaited the minorities. "Generous to a fault," he said and added "whatever might be the attitude of India. I hope Congress will be just as we of Pakistan are resolved upon a policy of generosity to the Hindus and other minorities. I am going to show how the minorities should be treated."[39] To another question he replied that he should unhesitatingly give the Hindu minorities in Pakistan all the privileges he had demanded for the Indian Muslims.[40]

Having established Pakistan on the basis of two-nation theory, Jinnah himself discarded it. He announced in the Constituent Assembly that Hindus and Muslims were not two nations but were two communities.

While inaugurating the first session of the Pakistan Constituent Assembly on August 11, 1947, he firmly declared: "You are free; you are free to go to your temples, you are free to go to your mosques or any other place of worship in this State of Pakistan. You may belong to any religion or caste or creed that has nothing to do with the fundamental principle that we are all citizens and equal citizens of one state.... Now I think, we should keep that in front of us as our ideal and you will find that in course of time, Hindus would cease to be Hindus, and Muslims would cease to be Muslims, not in the religious sense, because, that is the personal faith of each individual, but in the political sense of the citizens of the state."[41]

But he became handicapped by the very nature of the volcanic forces he had aroused. The fanatics tolerated Jinnah till Pakistan was achieved. Now, they did not require his services and Jinnah had no local base as he had been a Bombayite. Jinnah, the Governor-General, the Supreme Commander of Armed Forces, the President of the Constituent Assembly and the President of the Muslim League became the target both of paper propaganda and physical attack. If Jinnah had used them before partition, they had tolerated his utterings before Pakistan became a reality. Now they became determined to thwart all his desired moves and put stiff resistance. In the state of Pakistan, Jinnah and his like minded progressive and secular people were of no use to the obscurantist forces. Jinnah in such a state became a pathetic creature. His utterances in the Assembly, "raised such a storm of indignation, even among his own immediate followers that he had to propitiate them next day by offering 'Nimaz' publicly, something that he had never permitted himself to do throughout his political career."[42] Many parts of his speeches were not published by most of the newspapers in Pakistan.

He could make happy neither the communal nor the progressive minority forces. Humiliations, hurt and dejection had made him leave the Congress, never to join it again. But he suffered the same treatment at the hands of the leaders of the country of his own creation. These were the very people who, before partition could not dare to annoy and alienate him and had obeyed his orders like commandments.[43]

He had earned the hatred of all the Indians, Hindu, Muslim, Sikh alike. In his new country, he was cursed by the Muslim refugees who had left their homes and had come to Pakistan presuming life to be a bed of roses there. They felt betrayed. Within a week of the inauguration of Pakistan some Muslim refugees carrying lethal weapons, managed to enter into the Government House. They wanted to kill Jinnah but were overpowered.[44]

He had already forfeited the confidence of the minorities of Pakistan who had to pay the price of believing Jinnah that Pakistan would be a democratic state and their life and interests would be safeguarded and had stayed back. Their brutal butchery, loot, plunder, the dishonour of their women folk, the forcible conversion and the helpless condition of the old, moved even an iron man like Jinnah to tears. In one of the Hindu Refugee camps, he lost his nerve and wept.[45]

Thus the Protector General of the Hindu minority in Pakistan became himself a helpless creature. His patronage could not ensure the safety even of his dear friend Dalmia. He had to leave Pakistan. M.S.M. Sharma and Jogendera Mandal followed him soon.

Cut off from the best elements in Hindu society, with whose help alone in United India he could have given a determined fight to the mad Mullahs threatening to set the clock back, haunted by his own forces and inhibitions, blackmailed by the extremists in his own camp and overwhelmed by the 'revivalist mood' that always dominated a stricken people, the aged Quaid-e-Azam found himself a helpless prisoner in the topsy turvy world of his own creation.[46]

He became a pathetic creature. He couldn't undo his past. He wanted to come back to India. In fact, he considered himself to be an Indian. What a tragedy of a person like Jinnah. He died on September 11, 1948.

An in depth analysis of Jinnah's upbringing, training and outlook nay his personality as a whole—as has been brought out in this retrospect, establishes beyond doubt that he was never motivated in any of his actions all through his public life by love for Islam. Right from his childhood he had no involvement with his religion because the Aga Khani sect to which he and his family belonged had strong non-Islamic influence in its practices. Moreover, Jinnah had never shown any religious inclination. God had never interested him. He took up the cause of the Muslims only because it helped him politically; unfortunately Indian politics could never rise above its communal moorings. At first he aligned himself with the Hindus and worked incessantly for Hindu-Muslim unity. That established him as the best link between the two communities and gave him an added advantage in pursuing his brand of politics. Later, with the advent of Gandhi, the political environment changed and Jinnah was sidelined as a result of his aversion to mass agitation; he then concentrated all his energy in rebuilding his leadership by associating with the anti-Gandhi forces. Being a successful lawyer, he continued to be admired for his forensic abilities and brilliant advocacy. And although the Congress had grown averse to him, it could also not completely ignore him.

Nevertheless, in the latter part of his political career, he had indeed lost the clout that he earlier enjoyed; and that was basically on several counts: The generality of the Muslims felt alienated from him after he refused to support the Khilafat movement. Besides he was out of place with leaders who quoted the Quran and spoke in Urdu. He was ignorant of both. His whole being revolted against the domination of politics by the mullahs and the maulanas among the Muslims and the Mahatma and the pundits among the Hindus. He told Gandhi bluntly that his ways would bring nothing but ruin to the country. He tried to resurrect his leadership by making the League the instrument of his politics; but then the Organisation did not have the image nor the influence to enable him to do so. Because of Gandhi's support to the Khilafat movement, most of the politically minded Muslims continued to be with the Congress.

Though isolated, Jinnah did not give up his efforts to unite the Hindus and the Muslims to obtain constitutional reforms, safeguarding the interests of the Muslims. The worst blow that he suffered was the rejection of his amendments to the Nehru Report of 1928. Until then he had struggled unfailingly to arrive at a consensus on Hindu Muslim differences but now, under the changed circumstances, every move he made became suspect. At first, he was distrusted by the Hindus, but later even the Muslims doubted his motives. Besides, other Muslim leaders like the Aga Khan and Sir Fazl i Husain had meanwhile also appeared on the scene at that time and they managed to oust him. Consequently he was so disheartened that he decided to give up politics and retire in London. There too, he made futile efforts to find new political pastures by trying to enter the House of Commons.

Jinnah however could not rest content for long; his burning desire was to be in the limelight and this drove him to regain his position. He went back to India with a new determination. From an avowed nationalist, he became an arch communalist. He took an aggressively anti-Hindu stand and concentrated all his energies on mobilising the Muslims. He made it his mission to unite the Muslims and activate the moribund League. He became a born again Muslim hoping to rise on the convenient shoulders of communalism.

The task was not easy; he lacked the necessary cultural bearing to woo the Muslims. He had no emotional attachment to their sacred places nor to their customs, language and conventions. The nexus to connect with them was missing. He had no doubt fought for them in the past but he had done so by cooperating with the Hindus and working for a united front.

Later when he took to communal plank, he had to undo all that he had done in the past. In the process he discarded the Hindus but he could not totally align with the practising Muslims. He was too deeply entrenched in his western style of living and thinking to give it up. He could not easily mix with the illiterate Muslim masses; he felt comfortable only among the western educated elite. The poor and the downtrodden Muslims failed to interest him; even when he put on the exclusively communal garb and reorganised the League he relied more on the lordly nawabs and the rich and indolent jagirdars. Iqbal had cautioned him a year before his death in a letter dated May 28, 1937: "The League will have to finally decide whether it will remain a body representing the upper classes of Indian Muslims or Muslim masses.... The question therefore is: how is it possible to solve the problem of Muslim poverty? And the whole future of the League depends on the League's activity to solve this question. If the League can give no such promises I am sure the Muslim masses will remain indifferent to it as before."[47]

Jinnah did not however heed the poet's advice; he was mainly interested in building an exclusive platform for himself and within no time he managed to gather the Muslims under his leadership without changing either his thinking or his approach. His lack of knowledge of Islam and his inability to speak Urdu proved no hindrance. His contempt for the masses remained unchanged. An incident, which Rafiq Zakaria has narrated in his book, *Price of Partition* confirms it. It happened at the mammoth public meeting, which the League had organised to celebrate the Deliverance Day on the exit of the Congress ministries in 1939. "Just before the meeting Jinnah's behaviour startled me beyond comprehension. He arrived at the specified time. He was always punctual." He surveyed the scene and when he could not see the press seated prominently in the front rows, he lost his temper. He turned to the organisers and shouted angrily: "Where is the press?" and then in full hearing of the public since the mike was on the dais, he thundered: "Do you think I have come to address these donkeys?"[48] He wanted his speech to be conveyed more to the world than to the assembled crowd. Despite the handicap of being a Muslim and the arrogance in his approach he managed to become the darling of the Muslims. He exploited their religious leanings and inculcated in them the fear of Hindu domination. He coined the Two-Nation theory, cleverly stressing on the vital differences between Hindus and Muslims. He convinced Muslims that the Hindus would never share power with them. Their sole objective, he told them, was to oust the British, establish Hindu Raj and subjugate them, so as to avenge the alleged atrocities committed by the medieval Muslim rulers.

In building a new leadership for himself, on the basis of Muslim separatism that he had earlier abhorred, Jinnah deliberately ignored the various commonalities between Hindus and Muslims. In the earlier phase of his public life, he often spoke of how the two lived together peacefully for centuries despite some differences, even hostilities. In those days, he never let go an opportunity to emphasise that the two communities showed respect and consideration for one another and managed the contradictions in their relationship with goodwill and harmony. Their heroes and festivals, he said, might have been different but they never caused any major conflict on either side. There was a silent and peaceful acceptance of the diversities and differences in their approach on vital matters. Jinnah was then of the opinion that the so called Hindu Muslim riots were the products of the British Raj; during the Muslim rule, there might have been wars between Muslim and Hindu rulers, but there was never any discord between the ordinary people of the two communities. The elite might have at times experienced some tension and animosity among themselves but the people at large had always lived in peaceful co-existence.

Jinnah had sworn by these facts all along until the last seven or eight years of his life, but he brazenly denied them as he embarked on his new role as defender of the faithful. He then began propagating that there was little in common between Hindus and Muslims and that they could never live and work together. He misrepresented Gandhi's call for *Ram Rajya* among Muslims and asked them to demand a separate state for themselves. This earned him a positive response which helped him assume the role of their sole spokesman. He did not mind using any means to achieve this end. John Gunther in his celebrated work *Inside Asia* has commented: "His opposition to the Hindus is bitter and inflamed; he tours the country making attacks on Congress, which splits and weakens nationalist sentiment. Jinnah says that he was driven into communalism and the resurrection of the Moslem League by the intransigence of the Hindus, but his own intense political ambition had much to do with it."[49]

And thus he took charge of the League and mobilised the Muslims under its aegis and with his mesmerising technique, he galvanised them into a force to reckon with. He made himself so politically invulnerable that the British accepted him as the authentic representative of the Muslims and eventually the Congress too conceded that status to him, even if unwillingly. He felt truly elevated when he was equated with Gandhi. This was exactly what he had aimed for ever since he returned from London in the early thirties. He steadfastly pursued his objective to partition the country. He used every political means and organisational measure to counter his opponents and often had the better of them. He did not deviate from his armchair politics but still managed to win over the Muslim masses.

Sometimes when his detractors questioned him on what sacrifice he would be ready to make for the Muslims, he scoffed at them saying, he did not believe in aping Gandhi whose methods of non-cooperation and mass agitation he detested. He missed no opportunity to pour venom on the Congress and the Hindus and always kept the British on his side; within the League he was able to have complete sway. This he did surprisingly by maintaining a distance from all. He enjoyed being eulogised; his monumental ego brooked no opposition. He thrived on his command being unquestionably obeyed. His vanity was overbearing; he had contempt for all those who disagreed with him. In the evening of his life, when he was obsessed with his pet scheme of Pakistan, he had convinced himself that it was the solution. He refused to listen to any argument against it. Nor was he deterred by the mounting opposition unleashed by his opponents. The more they questioned him about the viability of Pakistan the more dogmatic he became in pursuing it.

Jinnah had, no doubt, used Islam to obtain his Pakistan but as soon as it came into existence he clarified that he would run the newly born state on modern, western lines. He was also not enamoured of the parliamentary system which he so often denounced. He was all for the presidential system though he did not spell it out. He believed in concentrating all powers in his own hands. He made that clear when he appointed himself as Governor-

General. He saw to it that the politicians who gathered round him, the bureaucrats who came to him, the colonels and generals who saluted him, followed his diktat. He ruled as the British viceroys did. That was the reason he retained the administrative set up of the colonial masters who loved pomp and pageantry and showed little interest in the welfare of the masses. Jinnah imitated their style of functioning and systematically discouraged every move to Islamise Pakistan. Those who succeeded him followed faithfully in his footsteps.

REFERENCES

1. Joachim, Alva, *Leaders of India* (Bombay: Thacker & Co.), 1943, p. 65.
2. Damodar P. Singhal, *Pakistan* (New Jersey: Prentice Hall), 1972, p. 170.
3. Binayandra Mohan Chaudhry, *Muslim Politics in India* (Calcutta: Orient Longman), 1946, p. 67.
4. *Ibid.*
5. Allen Hayes Merriam, *Gandhi vs Jinnah* (Calcutta: Minerva), 1980, p. 90.
6. *Ibid.*, p. 91.
7. V.P. Menon, *Transfer of Power*, Vol. VIII (New Delhi: Orient Longman), 1968, p. 673.
8. J.N. Sahni, *The Lid Off* (Bombay: Allied Publishers), 1971, p. 155.
9. *Ibid.*
10. M.R.A. Baig, *In Different Saddles* (New York: Asia Publications), 1967, pp. 135-36.
11. *Ibid.*
12. Aziz Beg, *Jinnah and His Times* (Islamabad: Babur & Amer), 1986, p. 36.
13. M.R.A. Baig, *In Different Saddles*, *op. cit.*, pp. 136-38.
14. *Ibid.*
15. Hector Bolitho, *Jinnah: Creator of Pakistan* (London: John Murray), 1954, p. 153.
16. *Ibid.*
17. K.H. Khurshid, *Memories of Jinnah* (Karachi: Oxford University Press), 1990, p. 12.
18. *Ibid.*, p. 62.
19. M.C. Chagla, *Roses in December* (Bombay: Bharatiya Vidya Bhawan), 1978, p. 80.
20. Shahid Hamid, *Disastrous Twilight* (Leo-Cooper: Oxford University Press), 1986, p. 219.
21. Penderel Moon, *Divide and Quit* (London: Chatto & Windus), 1964, p. 21.
22. Kanji Dwarkadas, *Ten Years to Freedom* (Bombay: Popular Prakashan), 1968, pp. 78-79.

23. Shahid Hamid, *Disastrous Twilight, op. cit.*, p. 101.
24. *The Indian Express*, Chandigarh, 9 August 2005.
25. H.V. Hudson, *The Great Divide* (Karachi: Oxford University Press), 1969, p. 229.
26. M.S.M. Sharma, *Peeps into Pakistan* (Patna: Pustak Bhandar), 1954, p. 147.
27. Wali Khan, *Facts are Facts—The Untold Story of Partisan* (New Delhi: Vikas Publications), 1987, pp. 135-137.
28. J.N. Sahni, *The Lid Off, op. cit.*, p. 290.
29. M.N. Roy, *Men I Met* (New Delhi: Lalvani Publications), 1968, p. 32.
30. *Ibid.*, p. 34.
31. K.K. Aziz, *Rahmat Ali—A Biography* (Lahore: Vanguard), 1987, p. 262.
32. *Ibid.*
33. H.M. Seervai, *Partition of India—Legend and Reality* (Bombay: Emmenem Publishers), 1989, p. 314.
34. Wali Khan, *Facts are Facts—The Untold Story of Partisan, op. cit.*, p. 158.
35. Sri Prakash, *Pakistan: Birth and Early Years* (Delhi: Meenakshi Prakashan), 1965, p. 37.
36. K.L. Gaba, *Inside Pakistan* (Delhi: Raj Kamal Publications), 1948, p. 80.
37. M.S.M. Sharma, *Peeps into Pakistan, op. cit.*, p. 136.
38. *Ibid.*, p. 137.
39. *Ibid.*
40. *Ibid.*
41. Constituent Assembly of Pakistan Debates, 11 August 1947, Vol. I, No. 2, pp. 18-20.
42. Hashoo Kewal Ramani, *Pakistan X-Rayed* (Delhi: New Age Publication), 1955, p. 5.
43. Ajeet Jawed, *Secular and Nationalist Jinnah* (New Delhi: Kitab Publishing House), 1998, pp 293-94.
44. M.S.M. Sharma *Peeps into Pakistan, op. cit.*, p. 146.
45. S.M. Ikram, *Modern Muslim India and the Birth of Pakistan* (Lahore: S.M. Ikram), 1965, p. 318.
46. Hashoo Kewal Ramani, *Pakistan X-Rayed, op. cit.*, p. 12.
47. Letters of Iqbal to Jinnah, published by Muhammad Ashraf quoted in Rafiq Zakaria, *The Man Who Divided Pakistan* (Mumbai: Popular Prakashan), 2002, p. 222.
48. Rafiq Zakaria, *Price of Partition* (Mumbai: Bharatiya Vidaya Bhawan), 1998, p. 39.
49. John Gunther, *Inside Asia* (New York: Hamilton), 1938, p. 486.

BIBLIOGRAPHY

Ahmad, Nazir, *Ibn ul Waqt* (Lahore: Sheikh Mubarak Ali), 1949.

Ahmad, Jamil-ud-Din (ed.), *Speeches and Writings of Mr. Jinnah*, Vol. I (Lahore: Ashraf), 1960.

Ahmed, Akbar S., *Jinnah, Pakistan and Islamic Identity* (Karachi: Oxford University Press).

Ahmad, Aziz, *Islamic Modernism in India and Pakistan 1857-1964* (London: Oxford University Press), 1967.

Ahmad, Rizwan (ed.) *The Quaid-e-Azam Papers* (Karachi: East & West Publishing Co.), 1976.

Ahmad, Rizwan (ed.) *Iqbal's Letters to Quaid-e-Azam* (Lahore: Friends Educational Service), 1966.

Akbar, Ahmad, *Jinnah Pakistan and Islamic Identity* (London: Routledge), 1997.

Almeida, Prakash, *Jinnah Man of Destiny* (Delhi: Kalpaz Publications), 2001.

Ambedkar, B.R., *Pakistan or the Partition of India* (Bombay: Thacker & Co.), 1946.

Ambedkar, B.R., *What Congress and Gandhi Have Done to the Untouchables* (Bombay: Thacker & Co.), 1946.

Azad, Maulana Abul Kalam, *India Wins Freedom* (Calcutta: Longmans), 1959.

Aziz, Beg, *Jinnah and His Time* (Islamabad: Babur and Amer Publications), 1986.

Aziz, K.K., *Rahmat Ali—A Biography* (Lahore: Vanguard), 1987.

Aziz, K.K., *The Making of Pakistan* (London: Chatto & Windus), 1967.

Bakshi, Illahi, *With Quiad-e-Azam During His Last Days* (Karachi: Quaid-e-Azam Academy), 1978.

Baig, M.R.A., *In Different Saddles* (New York: Asia Publications), 1967.

Bamford, P.C., *Histories of Non-Cooperation and Khilafat Movements* (New Delhi: Deep and Deep), 1974.

Bhardwaj, K.K., *Pakistan's March to Democracy and Liberalism* (New Delhi: Anmol Publications), 1996.

Bhutto, Zulfikar Ali, *The Myth of Independence* (London: Oxford University Press), 1969.

Blunt, W.S., *India Under Ripon: A Private Diary* (London: T. Fisher Unwin), 1909.

Bolitho, Hector, *Jinnah: Creator of Pakistan* (London: John Murray), 1954.

Bose, Subhash Chandra, *The Indian Struggle Part II* (Calcutta: Published for Netaji Publishing Society), 1945.

Buski, Shahid Javed, *Pakistan: The Continuing Struggle for Nationhood* (Boulder Colo. West View Press), 1991.

Chagla, M.C., *Roses in December: An Autobiography* (Bombay: Bharatiya Vidya Bhawan), 1978.

Chandra, Bipin, *Communalism in India* (New Delhi: Vani Educational Books), 1984.

Chandra, Bipin, *India's Struggle for Independence 1857-1947* (New Delhi: Viking), 1988.

Chandra, Bipin, *Modern India* (New Delhi: NCERT), 1976.

Chandra, Bipin, *Nationalism and Colonialism in Modern India* (New Delhi: Orient Longman's Ltd.), 1979.

Chaudhri, Khaliquzzaman, *Pathway to Pakistan* (Lahore: Pakistan Longman), 1961.

Chaudhry, Binayandra Mohan, *Muslim Politics in India* (Calcutta: Orient Longman), 1946.

Chaudhry, Kailash, *Tragedy of Jinnah* (Lahore: Varma Publishing Co.), 1943.

Chaudhary, Rahmat Ali, *Pakistan: The Farther Land of Pak Nation* (London: The Pak National Liberal Movement), 1947.

Chaudhry, Sandhaya, *Gandhi and Partition of India* (New Delhi: Sterling), 1984.

Chiral, Valentine, *India, Old and New* (New Delhi: Light and Life Publishers), 1975.

Chiral, Valentine, *The Indian Unrest* (New Delhi: Light and Life Publishers), 1979.

Cohen, Stephen Philip, *The Idea of Pakistan* (New Delhi: Oxford University Press), 2005.

Collins Larry and Dominique Lapierre, *Freedom at Midnight* (New Delhi: Vikas Publications), 1973.

Constituent Assembly of Pakistan Debates, 11 August 1947, Vol. I, No. 2, pp. 18-20.

Countess Mary of Minto, *India, Minto and Morely 1905-1910* (London: Macmillan), 1934.

Coupland, R., *The Indian Problem Part II* (New York: Oxford University Press), 1944.

Cunning John (ed.), *Political India 1832-1932* (London: Oxford University Press), 1932.

Damodar P. Singhal, *Pakistan* (New Jersey: Prentice Hall), 1972.

Das, Durga, *India from Curzon to Nehru and After* (New York: John Doby), 1970.

Datta, S.K. and Rajiv Sharma, *Pakistan from Jinnah to Jehad* (New Delhi: UBSPD), 2002.

Dodwell, H.H. (ed.), *The Cambridge History of the British Empire*, Vol. 5 (London: Cambridge University Press), 1932.

Dutt, R. *Palme, India: Today and Tomorrow* (London: Lawrence and Wishart), 1955.

Embree, Ainslie T., *Imaging India: Essays on Indian History* (London: Oxford University Press), 1989.

Faruqi, Zakir Hussain, *Muslim League Kiyyum*? (Bombay: Maktaha-Sultani), 1947.

Gaba, K.L., *Inside Pakistan* (Delhi: Raj Kamal Publications), 1948.

Gandhi, M.K., *An Autobiography or The Story of My Experiments with Truth* (Ahmedabad: Navajivan Publishing House), 1983.

Gandhi, M.K., *Hind Swaraj* (Ahmedabad: Navajivan Publishing House), 1982.

Gopal, S., *Selected Works of Jawaharlal Nehru*, Vol. I (New Delhi: Orient Longman), 1972.

Gunther, John, *Inside Asia* (New York: Hamilton), 1938.

Hamid, Shahid, *Disastrous Twilight* (Leo-Çooper: Oxford University Press), 1986.

Hassan, Javed, *India: A Study in Profile* (Rawalpindi: Army Book Service), 1990.

Hasan, S.S., Plain Mr. Jinnah: Selections from Quaid-e-Azam correspondence relating mainly to personal matters (Karachi: Royal Book Company), 1976.

Hudson, H.V., *The Great Divide* (Karachi: Oxford University Press), 1969.

Hussain, Azim, *Fazl-i-Husain* (Bombay: Longmans), 1946.

Iqbal Afzal (ed.), *Select Writings and Speeches of Maulana Mohamed Ali* (Lahore: Ashsaf), 1944.

Ikram, S.M., *Modern Muslim India and the Birth of Pakistan* (Lahore: S. M. Ikram), 1965.

Jain, M.S., *The Aligarh Movement: Its Origin and Development 1858-1906* (Agra: Sri Ram Mehra), 1965.

Jayakar, M.R., *The Story of My Life* Vol. II (Bombay: Asia Publishing House), 1959.

Jawed, Ajeet, *Secular and Nationalist Jinnah* (New Delhi: Kitab Publishing House), 1998.

Jinnah, Fatima, *My Brother* (Karachi: Quaid-e-Azam Academy), 1987.

Jinnah, M.A., *History of the Origin of Fourteen Points* (Bombay: n.d), (Australia: Flinders University).

Jinnah, M.A., *Speeches and Writings* (Lahore: Mustaffa), 1960.

Joachim, Alva, *Leaders of India* (Bombay: Thacker & Co.), 1943.

Kanji, Dwarkadas, *India's Fight for Freedom: An Eye Witness Story, 1913-37* (Bombay: Poplar Prakashan), 1960.

Kanji, Dwarkadas, *Ten Years to Freedom* (Bombay: Popular Prakashan), 1968.

Khan, Wali, *Facts are Facts—The Untold Story of Partition* (New Delhi: Vikas Publications), 1987.

Khurshid, K.H., *Memories of Jinnah* (Karachi: Oxford University Press), 1990.

Lentizion, Nehemia (ed.), *Conversion to Islam* (New York: Holmes and Meir), 1979.

Letters of Iqbal to Jinnah, published by Muhammad Ashraf quoted in Rafiq Zakaria, *The Man Who Divided Pakistan* (Mumbai: Popular Prakashan), 2002.

Malik, Hafeez (ed.), *Pakistan Founders' Aspirations and Todays Realities* (New York: Oxford University Press), 2001.

Mansergh, Nicholas, E.W.R. Lumby and Penderel Moon, *The Transfer of Power 1942-47* (London: Her Majesty Stationery Office), 1970-83.

Masani, R.P., *Dadabhai Naoroji* (New Delhi: Publications Division, Ministry of Information and Broadcasting, Government of India), 1960.

Mazumdar, A.K., *Advent of Independence* (Bombay: Bharatiya Vidya Bhawan), 1963.

Majumdar, B.B., *Indian Political Association and Reforms of Legislatures (1818-1917)* (Calcutta: Minerva), 1945.

Mazumdar, R.C.; Rayachaudhary, H.C. & Dutta, Kali Kumar, *An Advanced History of India* (Madras: Macmillan), 1963.

McGrath, Allen, *The Destruction of Democracy in Pakistan* (Karachi: Oxford University Press), 1972.

Menon, V.P., *Transfer of Power*, Vol. VIII (New Delhi: Orient Longman), 1968.

Merriam, Allen Hayes, *Gandhi vs Jinnah: The Debate Over the Pakistan of India* (Calcutta: Minerva), 1980.

Mirza, Humanyun, *From Plassey to Pakistan* (New York: University Press of America), 1999.

Mody, Hormi, *Pherozeshah Mehta* (New Delhi: Publications Division, Ministry of Information and Broadcasting, Government of India), 1963.

Mohan, Sulakshana, *Pakistan Under Musharraf* (New Delhi: Indian Publishers), 1999.

Moon, Penderel, *Divide and Quit* (London: Chatto & Windus), 1964.

Morley, John Viscount, *Recollections*, Vol. II (London: Macmillan), 1918.

Mustafa, Zubeida (ed.), *The South Asian Century: 1900-1999* (London: Oxford University Press), 2000.

Naidu, Sarojini (ed.), *Mohammad Ali Jinnah, An Ambassador of Unity; His Speeches and Writings* (Madras: Ganesh), 1918.

Nanda, B.R., *Gandhi, Pan-Islamism, Imperialism and Nationalism in India* (Bombay: Oxford University Press), 1989.

Nehru, Jawaharlal, *An Autobiography* (London: The Bodley Head), 1937.

Page, D., *Prelude to Pakistan* (Delhi: Oxford University Press), 1982.

Prashad, Rajendra, *India Divided* (Bombay: Kitabs), 1947.

Pirzada, Syed Sharifuddin, *Quaid-e-Azam Jinnah's Correspondence* (New Delhi: Metropolitan Book Company), 1981.

Pirzada, S.S. (ed.), *Foundations of Pakistan, All India Muslim League Documents 1906-1947* (New Delhi: Metropolitan Book Company), 1982.

Pirzada, Syed Sharifuddin, *Some Aspects of Qaid-e-Azam's Life* (Islamabad: National Commission on Historical and Cultural Research), 1978.

Pirzada, S.S. (ed.), *The Collected Works of Quaid-e-Azam Mohammad Ali Jinnah*, Vol. I (Karachi: East West Publishing), 1969.

Radhakrishnan, S. (ed.), *Mahatma Gandhi* (London: George Allen), 1949.

Ralhan, O.P. (ed.), *Hindu Mahasabha*, Vol. II (New Delhi: Anmol), 1997.

Ramani, Hashoo *Kewal, Pakistan X-Rayed* (Delhi: New Age Publication), 1955.

Rawlinson, H.G., *The British Achievements in India* (London: William Hodge), 1948.

Resolutions of the All India Muslim League from March 1941 to April 1942 (Delhi: All India Muslim League).

Robinson, F., *Separation Among Muslims* (Cambridge: Cambridge University Press), 1974.

Roy, M.N., *Men I Met* (New Delhi: Lalvani Publications), 1968.

Sahni, J.N., *The Lid Off* (Bombay: Allied Publishers), 1971.

Sarojini, *Speeches and Writings* (Madras: G.A. Natesan), 1945.

Sayeed, K.B. *Pakistan The Formative Phase 1857-1948* (London: Oxford University Press), 1968.

Sayed, Khalid, B., *Pakistan The Formation Phase* (London: Oxford University Press), 1968.

Sayed, Zaifullah and Samuel Baid, *Pakistan: An End Without a Beginning* (Delhi: Lancer International).

Sayed, K.B., *Pakistan: The Formative Phase 1857-1948* (London: Oxford University Press), 1968.

Sayid, M.H., *The Sound of Fury: A Political Study of Mohammad Ali Jinnah* (New Delhi: Akbar Publishing House), 1983.

Spear, Percival, *India Pakistan and the West* (London: Oxford University Press), 1958.

Sitaramayya, B. Pattabhi, *The History of Indian National Congress*, Vol. I, 1985-1935 (Bombay: Padma Publications), 1946.

Seervai, H.M., *Partition of India—Legend and Reality* (Bombay: Emmenem Publishers), 1989.

Sharma, Jai Narain, "Irreligious Jinnah Wanted A Religious Pak", *The Tribune*, Chandigarh, 6 July 1997.

Sharma, Jai Narain, *Power, Politics and Corruption: A Gandhian Solution* (New Delhi: Deep and Deep), 2004.

Sharma, M.S.M., *Peeps Into Pakistan* (Patna: Pustak Bhandar), 1954.

Sharma, Rashmi (ed.), *Sonia versus Vajpayee* (New Delhi: Deep and Deep), 2004.

Sharif, Al-Mujahid, *Qaide-e-Azam* (Delhi: Low Price Publications), 1993.

Sherwani, Latif Ahmad, *Pakistan Resolution to Pakistan* (Delhi: Daya Publishing House), 1985.

Sikander Hayat, *Pakistan Resolution Revisited* (Islamabad: National Institute of Historical and Cultural Research), 1999.

Singh, Anita Inder, *The Origin of the Partition of India 1936-47* (Bombay: Oxford University Press), 1987.

Sitaramayya, Pattabhi, *History of Indian National Congress* (Delhi: S. Chand & Co.), 1969.

Sri Prakash, *Pakistan: Birth and Early Days* (New Delhi: Meenakshi Publications), 1956.

Sri Prakash, *Pakistan: Birth and Early Years* (Delhi: Meenakshi Prakashan), 1965.

Suda, J.P., *Main Currents of Social and Political Thought in India*, Vol. III (Meerut: K. Nath & Co.), 1973.

Symonds, Richard, *Making of Pakistan* (London: Faber and Faber), 1950.

Tara Chand, *History of Freedom Movement in India* (New Delhi: Publications Division, Ministry of Information and Broadcasting, Government of India), 1962.

Tendulkar, D.G., *Mahatma*, 8 Vols. (New Delhi: Publications Division, Ministry of Information and Broadcasting, Government of India), 1958.

Varma, V.P., *Modern Indian Political Thought* (Agra: Luxmi Narain Agarwal), 1961.

Wells, Ian Bryant, *Jinnah's Early Politics Ambassador of Hindu Muslim Unity* (Delhi: Permanent Black), 2005.

Wolpert, Stanley, *Jinnah of Pakistan* (New York: Oxford University Press), 1984.

Wolpert, S., *Tilak and Gokhale: Revolution and Reform in the Making of Modern India* (Barkeley: University of California Press), 1961.

Zaidi, A.M. and Shaheda Zaidi (eds.), *The Encyclopedia of Indian National Congress,* Vol. IV, 1901-1905 (New Delhi: S. Chand & Co.), 1978.

Zakaria, Rafiq, *The Man Who Divided India* (Mumbai: Popular Prakashan), 2002.

Zakaria, Rafiq, *Price of Partition* (Mumbai: Bharatiya Vidaya Bhawan), 1998.

Zulfikar, G.H., *Pakistan: As Visualised by Iqbal and Jinnah* (Lahore: Bajm-e-Iqbal), 1989.

Index